Get
REAL.

“

IF YOU’RE LEADING AND NO ONE IS FOLLOWING YOU, then you’re only taking a walk.

Afghan proverb

Get REAL.

Get REAL.

Be the leader you were meant to be.

by Steve Charlton

Get REAL.

Published by The REAL. Leadership Consultancy

ISBN: 978-1-7395257-0-5 (paperback)
978-1-7395257-1-2 (ebook)

First published 2023

Cover design and illustration: Mark Terry, NEO, The Creative Business Agency
Page layout and production: Catherine Williams, Chapter One Book Design

Printed in the United Kingdom

DEDICATION

This is dedicated to everyone I've worked with over the last 30 years; to those who inspired me to step off the corporate treadmill, find a purpose in life and do what I love doing.

For my Mum (who sadly passed away before I finished this book), who instilled in me the discipline and determination to succeed, the golden rule of treating everyone equally and with respect, and the importance of family above anything else.

Finally this is dedicated to my wife McKenna for her unwavering support and steadfast belief in me, and my son Alexander for inspiring me to do better things. I hope I've made him proud.

CONTENTS

INTRODUCTION

INTRODUCTION

Anyone can lead. You might not see yourself as a leader, but everyone has it inside them to step up, make an impact and get results when they need to. Look at most parents, they're doing that on a daily basis. Look at what teachers and medical professionals do. During the Covid-19 pandemic, none of these people were given any coaching or encouragement, they just had to do it. They had to step up, take control and inspire – when many other 'leaders' were running around like headless chickens. It was these everyday leaders we looked up to for support. REAL. leaders who communicated with us, kept everything running and kept us safe. They're probably the last people to call themselves leaders, but the impact of what they do is obvious, they were – and are – leaders. And that's because they have those leadership qualities inside of them. We all do. You do, too.

But there's a problem. At the moment there is a very old-fashioned template for how a leader should act. Outdated rules and expectations for leadership that no longer work.

Everyone has leadership skills within them, but people struggle to step up because they don't want to be shoehorned into being something they're not. Because of that, many people have a hard time truly believing they could do it. It's what stops a lot of potential leaders – a lot of ordinary, everyday people – from even thinking they could lead. They think, 'Oh well, it never occurred to me that I could do that. I'm not good enough.' And, for me, that's quite upsetting.

In my opinion, *everyone* can lead in some way. I'm not saying that everyone should be a leader just because they have the skills, but I'm saying if you *want* to lead, if that's something you know you have to do, that's half the battle. And now is the perfect time to step into leadership. The industry is changing and there is a different path emerging. You don't have to follow that old-fashioned template. You don't have to fit into someone else's box. You can still be yourself and be a REAL. leader; all you have to do is lean into those inherent leadership qualities you have within you.

In 2020, I set up the REAL. Leadership Consultancy after a 25-year career working with some of the world's leading companies, recruiting and developing hundreds of people. I've always been curious about people and loved helping them develop, from those starting their careers to those looking to become the next company CEO or president. Along the way I found that the people with the greatest potential to be incredible leaders were the ones who had four key traits (or pillars): Results, Empathy, Authenticity and Learning. It's not that some people had these and some didn't, it's just that those who focused and worked on improving these four traits were the ones most likely to become great leaders.

In this book I'm going to show you how to do just that. First I'll explain what the four key pillars are and why they are important. Then I'll show you how you can dial up each one so you can become a better leader. At the end of each point you'll see some numbered 'Actions' or a 'Thinking Point' – indicated by a spotlight icon. I've included these to help you apply the ideas to your own situation and to get you started putting these suggestions into action. Interspersed with the pillars, we look at other key leadership traits (such as Change, Purpose and Awareness). As a leader you have to make hundreds of decisions a day and you're often making them on the go, with little information. By reading this book, I want to provide you with some reassurance around that. I'll talk about the typical things you might worry about in a day and what you can do about that. You'll learn how to use the skills you already have, why you can't do it alone, when to step up and when to take a step back, and how to lead when it's all going wrong.

This book is not for you if you want a list to tick off, or an assessment to fill in to validate your leadership skills. I don't believe that to be a good leader you should fit into a specific mould. To me it's about recognising why you lead, how people experience your leadership and thinking about where you want to improve it. And it's not always about working on weaknesses, it's about improving your strengths, too.

You'll read examples from genuine clients and friends of mine (I've changed their names for anonymity). They've been included to show you that you aren't alone in these challenges.

As well as sharing my insights, advice and practical steps to becoming a leader, you'll see that I'll be challenging the traditional notion of leadership. That's why you'll find interviews from ordinary, everyday leaders – those who don't consider themselves as such – in this book. I'll challenge old-fashioned ideas of leadership and throw out some outdated methods. I want to prove to you that leadership comes in many forms, not just what you see and hear about in the media. So, if this sounds like a book for you, let's get started.

“

LEADERSHIP IS A BIT LIKE SWIMMING, YOU CAN'T LEARN IT FROM BOOKS. Ultimately, you have to get in the water.

—Henry Mintzberg

REAL. PILLARS

REAL. PILLARS

Leadership isn't easy. It's not something you can 'hack'. And the idea that there is only one set of 'behaviours' that leads to success is dated; what works for one leader will not work for another. The Covid-19 pandemic threw the rulebook out of the window and made everything personal – it made business personal. You couldn't just run a business during the pandemic without worrying about your people and what was going on with them.

Today, you have to embrace the people you lead, you have no choice. You have to care. If you don't care, you can't manage, you can't lead and you can't make an impact. This is the new type of leadership – what I call 'REAL. Leadership'.

To be a leader today of course, you still have to have the typical leadership characteristics like being competent, being a good communicator, having charisma (and a lot of other words that begin with the letter C). But there are four areas of focus that I've noticed the best leaders focus on and constantly work on improving – they also make up the REAL. leaders I'll be talking about in this book. They are Results, Empathy, Authenticity and Learning. Let's look at each of these traits briefly before we dive in.

RESULTS

So, what do I mean by 'Results' as a trait you can lean into? If you think about it, any leadership role is about getting results. If you're in this role, it's because you have the skills to achieve them. Either someone has seen that skill in you and hired you as a leader, or you've got there on your own. Being charismatic, being competent and well-respected is all part of being a great leader, but if you don't *achieve* anything – like hitting a target or meeting a deadline – it's pointless. Getting results means you're making an impact in some way, and that comes first as a leader. You're there to create success and to make things happen. But *how* you make that happen is where some leaders struggle. As you'll see in this book, skills like communication, taking initiative, self-awareness and recognising your team will fall under 'Results'. These are some of the skills you'll need to be aware of, and maybe work on, in order to get those results.

What that result is, will differ for each person. For some, getting those results means creating an impactful team. For others it will be hitting those numbers. Or it might be as simple as having opportunities to be creative. But there's a lot more to getting results than you might think.

EMPATHY

REAL. leaders care, it's essential. In 2020, emotional intelligence – which includes empathy, self-awareness and self-regulation – was ranked at number five in LinkedIn's annual list of the most in-demand soft skills[1] for the first time ever. What used to be considered a 'soft' skill is now vital, and there has never been a

1 LinkedIn's annual list of the most in-demand soft skills: https://www.linkedin.com/business/learning/blog/learning-and-development/most-in-demand-skills-2020

better time for empathetic leadership. Given what everyone went through during the pandemic, and the economic uncertainty we're currently in, you're not going to last long if you don't show empathy as a leader.

Embedding empathy into any workplace or group environment needs to come from the top down. Being the loudest in the room, ignoring the well-being of your people, or being cut-throat are old-fashioned practices we need to leave behind. You'll risk disenfranchising people who don't fit that particular mould. REAL. leadership is empathetic and people focused. You must make it clear that people come first and set the example that understanding different perspectives is not only important to your particular situation, but also creates success.

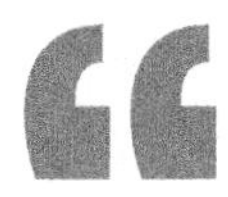

YOU CAN CARVE YOUR OWN PATH, BE YOUR OWN KIND OF LEADER. We do need to create a new generation of leadership.

—Jacinda Ardern, former New Zealand Prime Minister

AUTHENTICITY

Authenticity is closely linked to empathy as it's about being your true self and being honest with who you are. A lot of leaders feel like imposters because they don't fit that old-fashioned blueprint of what leadership should be. I believe that you should lead in a way that is most authentic to you, whatever that looks like. If you're going to attract great people into your workplace, if you want people to follow you, then you have to be an authentic leader. And the time for authenticity is now.

People are much more astute now about leaders. They expect more and are looking for leadership they can trust; they want sincere leaders who treat everyone fairly and equally.

The best leaders are honest, transparent and constantly communicate with their teams. They stay true to their personal and their organisation's values and inspire others with their vision.

LEARNING

This is probably the most important trait to develop. You've got to be learning all the time. Just because you're in a leadership position, you can't think you know everything. The best leaders have the humility to be constantly learning from everyone, even the most junior in an organisation, and have the confidence to admit 'I don't know'. They are keen to develop individuals to achieve their ambitions and openly encourage people to challenge them.

Learning drives innovation and change and the best leaders have a constant desire to improve. Some do that through simply reading, for others it's networking, taking professional development courses or coaching. The most effective leaders know they've got to be creative and agile, because that's how you survive uncertainty and change. In the current world the best leaders are learning as they go, adapting as necessary and, most importantly, listening and learning from those around them.

PEOPLE POWER

There is one overarching focus that no leader can hide from: power has shifted to the people. By being a more empathetic, authentic and results-focused leader, who is learning all the time, you will achieve success. And you can do so in a way that will still allow your other traits to shine through. You're still going to have all those other leadership skills, other things you're good at that make you a great leader, but those four pillars – Results, Empathy, Authenticity and Learning – are what I want you to focus on. I'll show you how.

EVERYDAY LEADERS

EVERYDAY LEADERS

Before we dive into the pillars, I want to tell you about a trolley attendant. It was within days of a UK lockdown starting during the pandemic, and there was a period of frustration and confusion as everyone tried to navigate the new shopping restrictions. I was at my local supermarket and I saw this attendant having to marshal frustrated shoppers outside the door, and deal with situations he would never have dreamed of, or indeed trained for. Yet he stayed calm, used humour and showed leadership capabilities that many other leaders could only hope to display. It was inspiring. He probably wouldn't have considered himself a leader, but he had it in him.

Before I started writing this book, I knew I wanted to profile people like that. I didn't want to focus on CEOs, politicians or typical business leaders; there are enough leadership books about them. I wanted to focus on people who had become leaders by accident or because of circumstance. I want you to be able to recognise yourself in the people I talk about, which is why I interviewed the following six people to include in this book. They probably never planned on being leaders, but have since found they have leadership qualities and have put them to good use. I want you to see that all leaders have the same challenges and problems as each other, no matter who they are or what they do.

DR. EUNICE NDIRANGU-MUGO

Dr. Eunice studied nursing in Kenya before getting a Master's in Advanced Nursing Practice and a PhD in Nursing Studies from The University of Nottingham. Her work focuses on topics such as infectious diseases (HIV/AIDS), well-being, adolescent health, health policy and higher education. She is the Chair of the Nursing Council of Kenya and maintains roles as a board member of One Girl Can and a Lead of other organisations related to nursing and midwifery.

ALEX STEPHANY

Alex originally trained in law, before moving into the technology sector and startups and becoming the CEO of JustPark. After making friends with a homeless man who would sit outside his local train station, Alex was inspired to create Beam, an award-winning crowdfunding platform for homeless people.

PETE WALLROTH

Pete worked in the housing sector and was a regeneration officer in Manchester. His role was to be a friendly face in his local community and help people find opportunities for change. In 2013 he founded Mummy's Star, a charity dedicated to supporting women and birthing people diagnosed with cancer during pregnancy or within 12 months of giving birth, and their families.

MICKELA HALL-RAMSAY

Mickela comes from a sports background and competed for Haringey at the London Youth Games between 2000 and 2004, winning gold in basketball. She is now the founder and director of the HR Sports Academy, a Community Interest Company dedicated to empowering children and young people with valuable life skills and sporting opportunities. She is also a trustee/board member of the London Youth Games, Europe's largest youth sports festival.

MARC CONVEY

After suffering life-changing burns at the age of 14, Marc was forced to see life differently. After working in the poker industry he became the co-founder and CEO of 23D, a media production company. Now, he is the co-founder of Thrive Now, a social enterprise promoting positive change for the planet.

CARLOS ANDRES POSADA LOPEZ

Carlos started out as a mechanical engineer specialising in sustainable energy systems. He had an interest in the sustainable energy market and agriculture and worked with a variety of different industries such as construction, oil and gas, and food processing. He founded Quo Agro Justo, a sustainable agri-tech business in Colombia that supports local farmers and helps them to connect with wholesalers, with an emphasis on sustainability and fair wages. He is also a consultant for the Carbon Trust.

LET'S GO

It doesn't matter where you started or where you are now. It doesn't matter what your journey to leadership looks like, or if you're still figuring it out. There is no blueprint for leadership. You don't have to be like the leaders you saw growing up, and I'm not saying you have to be anything like the people I'm going to refer to in this book. But I truly believe that anyone can lead, and the advice in this book will help you get there. So, if it's all right with you, let's get started with Pillar 1: Results.

RESULTS

“

Leadership is **THE ART OF GETTING PEOPLE TO WANT TO DO WHAT MUST BE DONE.**

—Jim Collins

RESULTS

1. WHAT DOES SUCCESS MEAN TO YOU?

Success is about the impact you want to make. Think back to the teachers or medical professionals during the Covid-19 pandemic. Think about people you know who don't have the label of a 'leader', and yet are able to step up when needed. They won't see themselves as leaders, but if you think about it, they're still having an impact on the people around them. Whether they're therapists, business managers, caregivers or construction workers, they're all still getting things done and inspiring people around them. It's not always about business results, it's about the impact of what you do.

Everyone has to have something they can look back on and say 'I've achieved that'. You may think you're not results-focused or competitive, but if you're responsible for the success of *something* or *someone,* and achieving that makes you feel good, then that might be your definition of success.

So, how are you going to validate success? Will it be numbers on a piece of paper or is it something that people say? For some, it's their family saying 'I'm proud of you'. There are lots of different ways to validate it for yourself; it doesn't have to be professional, it can be personal, too. If you're struggling, think about what you *don't want to be.* Or what you *don't want to be doing* in 12 months' time. Framing it that way can make you more definitive with your answers. Rather than saying you want a better work/life balance, commit to not working after 6pm to spend more time with your family.

People say to me, 'You must be so happy that you're working for yourself.' But to me, that's not my goal. To me it's more about the impact. I want more people saying, 'That was really helpful', or 'That really works'. And a lot of the time, I get the most impact from the people that aren't even paying me. That's what my result is; that's what success means to me. What does success mean for you?

STEP 1. DEFINE WHAT SUCCESS REALLY MEANS TO YOU, WHETHER PROFESSIONALLY OR PERSONALLY.

STEP 2. UNDERSTAND AND BE CLEAR ON WHY THIS IS *YOUR* DEFINITION OF SUCCESS.

STEP 3. FIND WAYS TO RECOGNISE IT WHEN YOU'VE ACHIEVED IT. IS IT SOMETHING PEOPLE SAY OR SOMETHING YOU CAN MEASURE?

2. REVIEW YOUR PERSONAL TIMELINE

A few years' ago I was at a corporate coaching event, and I was given an exercise that changed the way I viewed everything: how I viewed myself, how I was leading – everything.

On a blank piece of paper, I was told to draw a timeline. And on that timeline I was to mark down the positive and negative moments that had happened in my life, everything that I could remember from when I was a young child up to today. So, I marked down events like getting my first job, my parents splitting up, going to university – the events that shaped who I was today. Looking at that timeline, I soon realised when I first developed one of my negative traits. It was around the time my parents split up and I had to step up and help care for my brothers. As a leader, being nurturing and empathetic came quite naturally to me, but trust is something I struggle with and I don't like authority; I don't like being managed. This made me aware of exactly where I could improve.

Having this level of self-awareness will help you better manage your leadership style, navigate uncertainty and help you create the results you want. You'll feel good about what you've achieved, how you've grown and confirm what leadership traits you already have. It's a good way to discuss your leadership role-models and who you think about when you're in a tough situation – as well as who you want to avoid becoming. But it'll also show you how those people and past experiences have shaped the way you lead today. If you're habitually defensive about something, then work out why that is. If you're always working until you burn out, find out where that started.

This exercise made me see that I was actually quite sick of sitting in meetings and knowing what everyone was going to say before they opened their mouths. I didn't want to turn into my father, who had been frustrated by not achieving his ambitions. I wanted to have a personal purpose in life and have no regrets. I wanted to prove to my son that everyone has choices in life and you don't have to be stuck doing something you don't enjoy. You should always be brave enough to follow your dreams. Having this level of self-awareness can be uncomfortable at first, but the answers you'll find will help you navigate the challenges you'll face as a leader in the future.

STEP 1. **GET A PIECE OF PAPER, DRAW A TIME-LINE, AND MARK DOWN THE POSITIVE AND NEGATIVE EVENTS THAT HAVE HAPPENED TO YOU. GO AND TALK TO OTHER PEOPLE, FRIENDS AND RELATIVES TO HELP YOU FILL IN THE GAPS. (YOU CAN DO THIS THE OTHER WAY ROUND, TOO, WHERE YOU WRITE DOWN YOUR TRAITS AND THINK BACK CHRONOLOGICALLY OVER THE YEARS.)**

STEP 2. **LOOK FOR THOSE EVENTS THAT HAVE IMPACTED THE WAY YOU LEAD. WAS IT YOUR UPBRINGING? WAS IT YOUR FIRST JOB AND THE HORRIBLE BOSS YOU VOWED NEVER TO BE LIKE? WAS IT THE TIME YOU WENT TRAVELLING?**

STEP 3. **DON'T SEE THIS AS A ONE-OFF EXERCISE. KEEP COMING BACK TO IT AS YOU CHANGE AND GROW AS A LEADER. DEVELOPING SELF-AWARENESS IS AN ONGOING RESPONSIBILITY.**

3. FIND OUT WHAT THEY REALLY THINK

Leadership isn't about you, it's about them. It's about how people experience you. That's what leadership really is. Leaders of the past wanted to be bulletproof. They didn't want to be seen to be asking for help or advice, least of all from the people in their team. But times have changed and I think that's why a lot of traditional leaders are struggling at the moment.

Every time I suggest to a client that we find out what the team thinks, there's always this sharp intake of breath: 'Do we really have to do this? Can I cope with what they say?'

I've done this over the years myself and, honestly, the first few times I dreaded doing it. In your mind you're doing great, maybe you're getting the results you've been hired to achieve. But the reality is you might not be the leader you think you are. You might discover you're very money-oriented or you tend to avoid tough discussions. Perhaps you don't communicate effectively and people feel it's compromising your leadership.

One of my clients, Michael, thought he was a terrible leader. He was convinced his team hated him. But when he hired me to talk to them I found out they had a completely different impression of him. They totally understood why he was stressed and they could see he was beating himself up. His team were totally empathetic to his challenges and didn't think he was a terrible leader at all.

There will always be gaps between the way you *think* you lead, the way you *want* to lead and the way *people experience your leadership.* To be an effective leader you need to find out the answers to these questions, as well as your strengths and weaknesses. Yes, you might be getting the results, but is that really enough to be a REAL. leader?

“

ALL LEADERS, EVEN THE GOOD ONES, CAN SOMETIMES LOSE THEIR WAY AND BECOME SELFISH AND POWER-HUNGRY … they can sometimes forget that their responsibility as a leader is to their people.

—Simon Sinek

STEP 1. **IF YOU'VE GOT A GREAT RELATIONSHIP WITH YOUR TEAM, AND YOU KNOW THEY CAN BE HONEST WITH YOU, ASK THEM FOR FEEDBACK.**

STEP 2. **UNDERSTAND THAT THIS IS AN ONGOING PART OF BECOMING AN EFFECTIVE LEADER. KEEP CHECKING IN AND REVIEWING YOUR PERFORMANCE.**

STEP 3. **IF YOU DON'T HAVE A TEAM AROUND YOU THAT CAN BE HONEST WITH YOU, USE FORMS AND ASSESSMENTS THEY CAN FILL IN ANONYMOUSLY.**

STEP 4. **ALTERNATIVELY, BRING IN AN EXTERNAL EXPERT TO TALK TO YOUR TEAM AND GATHER THE RESULTS. IF YOU GET THE RIGHT PERSON TO ASK THE RIGHT QUESTIONS IN THE RIGHT WAY YOU WILL GET FAR BETTER FEEDBACK, TOO.**

4. LEADERS CREATE THE CULTURE

What do we mean by culture? Most dictionary definitions talk about the atmosphere, the behaviours and attitudes, but I also think it's the difference between what you say and what you do, how you stay true to your values.

And culture comes from the top; as a leader you are responsible for the direction that culture takes. From the types of people you recruit, to your communications, to any external facing part of your work. It's believed that almost 40% of an organisation's culture is influenced by its leadership.

Once, I was in a role where I had 150 people reporting to me and I discovered that I had this reputation for really chasing people up if they didn't reply to my messages. It wasn't that I wanted them to act on the email, I just wanted the validation that they'd received the message. If they didn't respond I assumed I'd done something wrong, so I created a calendar to remind myself to chase them up.

After speaking to a few trusted people in my team, someone told me it was just about communication: 'Tell people, "I might send you an email but I'm not looking to you to respond to it right there. But, if you don't mind, just send me a quick thumbs up or something, just so I know you've got it."'

To me, it felt like a selfish thing to do, to make that one of the behaviours I wanted on this team. But it actually translated quite well; that small change helped to develop a culture that took the pressure off people responding to emails outside work hours or when they were busy.

If your purpose is to do better for the world, then how does that translate into the kind of place you're going to lead? To the types of people you're going to bring in? What kinds of behaviours do you want to see? Does everyone fully understand why they are there? Are you looking for entrepreneurial people or those that prefer a team environment? You need to know what your culture is going to be.

A strong culture will continue to influence people's behaviours, even when no one is watching. What kind of culture do you want to create?

STEP 1. **GO BACK TO WHY THE BUSINESS WAS SET UP AND WHY YOU ARE A PART OF IT.**

STEP 2. **WHAT IS IMPORTANT TO YOU AND HOW IS THAT MANIFESTING IN THE BEHAVIOURS AND VALUES OF THE PEOPLE YOU WORK WITH?**

STEP 3. **LOOK AT THE PEOPLE AROUND YOU AND DECIDE IF THEY FIT INTO THAT CULTURE – THAT INCLUDES CLIENTS AS WELL AS STAFF. DOES ANYTHING, OR ANYONE, NEED TO CHANGE?**

5. WINS OVER AWARDS

Getting results doesn't always have to be about hitting the numbers. It could be as simple as some people doing great work together.

In the current complicated climate, where there's a lot of negativity and anxiety in the world, celebrating the little things together as a team is really important. Some people will be motivated by awards. They will want to know how they're doing and handing out awards will make them feel recognised. But don't forget about the people who might not always be so competitive, who aren't driven by a win, or by the recognition. They will be just as essential to your team, so you'll have to dig deeper and find some advice on how you can celebrate those people, too.

Create your own version of the People's Choice Awards, where the team votes for their favourite 'celebrities', much like the real public vote in the US. Hand out awards to people who the rest of the team value. As a leader you don't often see what's going on within your team, and you don't always know who is really stepping up and supporting others. So from that point of view, you might find something like this really valuable.

STEP 1. **FIND SMALL, AS WELL AS BIG, WINS TO CELEBRATE. WINS THAT PEOPLE MIGHT NOT TRADITIONALLY THINK IS A WIN – A GREAT CLIENT TESTIMONIAL, OR A WORK ANNIVERSARY, FOR EXAMPLE.**

STEP 2. **WHAT YOU VALUE AND WHAT YOUR TEAM VALUES MIGHT BE DIFFERENT. MAKE AN EFFORT TO FIND OUT WHO YOUR TEAM VALUES AND CELEBRATE THEM.**

STEP 3. **DON'T OVERLOOK THE PEOPLE WHO AREN'T ALWAYS ON THE FRONT LINE.**

6. INITIATIVE

Having initiative is one of the most important attributes a leader can have. It doesn't matter if you think you're a leader or not; if you can take the time to think, use a bit of judgement and act, you can do it.

It's not a big deal to take initiative, either. It's simply about deciding to do something and then getting on with it. In terms of taking initiative, I think there are a lot of everyday 'non-leaders' guiding the way, while still embodying everything we want from good leaders such as being flexible, creative and empathetic. Just look at the doctors and nurses who were making decisions on the fly, often in horrendous conditions, during the pandemic.

At the same time if you're always looking for the latest shiny thing, and you jump on every latest trend, that's just as bad. A leader who's too impulsive and chaotic isn't taking initiative because they've still got to weigh up the cost of each decision, too. What will be the cost to your team if you make that decision? Who will benefit? Is this worth it? It reminds me of the ripple effect. When you throw a small pebble into a pond, at first the ripples are small but then as they spread out they become larger. Every decision you make ripples out to your team and your company and sometimes leaders don't realise the impact of their actions, however well intended. You've got to find that balance.

And always consider *who* needs to be involved in making decisions – I've worked with organisations where the CEO has to sign off a new starter's email access, and been in a global board meeting where the main topic was how competent the office manager was!

If you don't show any initiative, then you're going to struggle as a leader. People underestimate how important this is. Decision-making under pressure can be paralysing, and people want to follow courageous leaders who aren't afraid to push forward. And especially in the environment right now, where there is no playbook, no one knows what the right solution is. You've just got to get on and do something; move your team, your ideas, your organisation forward.

“

WHEN YOU THROW A SMALL PEBBLE INTO A POND,
at first the ripples are small ... like every decision you make.

"

IN ANY MOMENT OF DECISION, THE BEST THING YOU CAN DO IS THE RIGHT THING, THE NEXT BEST THING IS THE WRONG THING,
and the worst thing you can do is nothing.

—Theodore Roosevelt

STEP 1. **TAKE TIME TO THINK OVER YOUR DECISION. WHAT'S THE CONTEXT AND IS THIS THE RIGHT OPPORTUNITY? GET ADVICE, SPEAK TO TRUSTED COLLEAGUES AND MAKE SURE YOU HAVE THE FULL PICTURE.**

STEP 2. **IT'S ALL ABOUT CONTEXT. IF YOU'RE A NEW LEADER BROUGHT IN TO MAKE CHANGE, THEN INITIATIVE IS GREAT. BUT IF YOU'VE BEEN BROUGHT IN TO STEADY THE SHIP, YOU HAVE A DIFFERENT CHALLENGE.**

STEP 3. **NO ONE CAN EVER REALLY KNOW IF THEY'VE MADE THE RIGHT DECISION, BUT AS LONG AS YOU DON'T SET IT IN STONE, YOU CAN ALWAYS ADAPT IT LATER.**

RESULTS
CHANGE

CHANGE

1. LEADING CHANGE

It's easy to lead when everything is going well. It's when it's going badly that you earn your money; your job is to get things back on track.

When my clients say, 'I'm finding it really difficult to manage, the numbers are down, it's getting tough,' I say to them, 'Isn't that brilliant? Because you're the leader and that's what you're paid to do.'

To be a REAL. leader you've got to be able to deal with changes. I think leadership of the future is something that is more adaptable, creative and innovative. These are essential qualities, rather than 'nice to haves' for today's leaders.

Mickela Hall-Ramsay remembers that when the pandemic happened, her leadership changed from the day-to-day tasks to more people-focused leadership; checking in with her staff and asking how they were coping. Pete notes that his charity is constantly evolving; every time they support a new family it creates a 'minuscule change in the pattern of support'. This constant evolution means it makes it much easier to collaborate and be open to support and ideas from external sources.

When you're leading through change, everything comes from the top. You can have people around you that implement the change, you can delegate, but if you want to make a success of change, it starts with you – because you're the leader. You've got to champion it and lead by example.

If you say you're going to create a workplace that's more client-facing, then as a leader you've got to be doing that, too. It amazes me how many people in leadership talk about having great communication, but on social media they never post anything, they don't communicate (and I just think that that's such a missed opportunity, especially in the connected world we're in today). Don't be afraid to mix up your teams, introduce new faces, or remove some old ones. It's going to take time, it's going to be bumpy and people will push back. This is normal. But your job as a leader is to make things happen.

STEP 1. OVER-COMMUNICATE CHANGE. TALK ABOUT WHAT'S HAPPENING, WHY YOU'RE MAKING CHANGES AND WHAT TO EXPECT.

STEP 2. EMBRACE THAT IT WILL TAKE TIME, BUT THIS PERIOD OF CHANGE WILL COME TO AN END.

STEP 3. BE EMPATHETIC. PEOPLE DON'T LIKE CHANGE BECAUSE IT'S CHANGE. IT'S SCARY. GIVE PEOPLE TIME TO ACCEPT CHANGE AT THEIR OWN SPEED.

Leading change also means being courageous, learning and adapting. It doesn't mean changing something for the sake of it. Your team will be sitting there thinking, 'Why are we doing this? What's the point?' Don't change just to keep things 'fresh' or to keep people on their toes, or because I've told you to. Every change you implement has to have a valid reason behind it.

If you are making changes I suggest following the Tuckman model. It's one I've used a number of times and is simple to use.

2. CHANGE WHEN THINGS ARE GOING WELL

Great leadership doesn't have to adapt to changes, it can create them, too. Don't be afraid to create change if you need to.

Think about where you or your workplace wants to be in 12 or in 18 months' time. There is a journey between where you are now and where you need to go. What skills do you need to develop to get there? Which people do you need to have around you? What will your organisation look like?

Even when things are going well, don't be afraid to shake it up and make the changes necessary to reach those goals. But don't just do it for the sake of it. Yes, it can be risky, and sometimes it might not always be successful. But when people are in a dynamic environment, with a leader that is constantly innovating, being creative and trying new things, it can be incredibly compelling and inspirational for them.

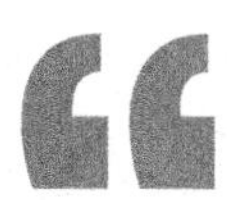

TURNING GOOD INTO GREAT TAKES ENERGY, but the building of momentum adds more energy back into the pool than it takes out.

—Jim Collins

For me, it's something that leaders should be thinking about and doing all the time. Keep finding ways to challenge the status quo and make changes to keep driving forward.

THE PEOPLE THAT GOT YOU TO WHERE YOU ARE TODAY PROBABLY WON'T GET YOU TO WHERE YOU WANT TO BE TOMORROW. TO HELP YOU SEE WHERE CHANGE NEEDS TO BE MADE, DO THE FOLLOWING SIMPLE EXERCISE WITH PEOPLE YOU CAN TRUST TO BE IMPARTIAL AND OBJECTIVE.

STEP 1. **MAP OUT THE STRUCTURE AND ROLES THAT YOU NEED, BUT DON'T INCLUDE ANY NAMES FROM YOUR CURRENT TEAM.**

STEP 2. **IDENTIFY THE SKILLS AND COMPETENCIES YOU NEED FOR EVERY ROLE AND HIGHLIGHT THE CRITICAL ROLES.**

STEP 3. **FINALLY, MAP YOUR CURRENT TEAM AGAINST THE STRUCTURE. WHO STAYS, WHO NEEDS TO GO AND WHO NEEDS DEVELOPMENT?**

3. STEPPING UP INTO LEADERSHIP

At the time of writing this book, one of my clients, Brendan, is stepping up from his team to become a leader. He and his best friend were in the same team and both applied for the job, but he got it.

Moving from being one of the team to leading the team is a challenge, but it doesn't have to be difficult. If this is you, be ready to have some awkward conversations at the start. Set boundaries between personal and professional – when does one stop and the other start? – and let your old team-mates know there will be times when you'll have to be tough on them. And know there will be times when they'll do the same to you. You may also have to fire people you were once working closely with.

But if you start by having an honest conversation and you've agreed those boundaries, be consistent. You can't suddenly fall back into being one of the team and ask for the latest gossip. Once you've decided to be a leader, you can't have it both ways.

This is not to say you can't stay friends with people, but there will be times they overstep, and times you will, too. You've got to focus on consistently keeping those personal/professional boundaries.

Of course you'll have worries. Are your friends talking about you and judging? Are you going to make a mistake? People will be watching you for evidence of any favouritism. What *will* help is to understand *why* you were given that role. Talk to your boss and find out why you were chosen so the next time you are challenged by your previous peers, you can back up your actions.

Sometimes you'll just have to front it out; not every meeting or situation is going to go well. If someone challenges you, don't overreact. But make sure you follow up and clear the air afterwards and don't beat yourself up about what you said or did. The reality is you can't be perfect all the time and you will make mistakes. Some of my best recruits have been those with the personality and drive for learning, and often they'd come from some of the most junior roles in other teams. As long as you rectify and learn, and stay on top of those people who cross the line, you'll be OK.

STEP 1. HAVE THOSE IMPORTANT CONVERSATIONS WITH YOUR OLD COLLEAGUES AND SET BOUNDARIES.

STEP 2. AGREE WHEN YOU WILL BE TALKING ABOUT PERSONAL ISSUES AND WHEN IT WILL BE ALL PROFESSIONAL; AGREE HOW YOU WILL CALL EACH OTHER OUT WHEN ONE OVERSTEPS THE BOUNDARIES.

STEP 3. UNDERSTAND WHY YOU WERE GIVEN THAT ROLE AND USE THOSE FACTS TO SUPPORT YOU WHEN YOU FEEL UNCERTAIN ABOUT YOUR LEADERSHIP.

STEP 4. DON'T EXPECT TO BE A PERFECT LEADER. KEEP LEARNING AND COMMUNICATING, AND STICK TO YOUR BOUNDARIES.

4. DARE TO BE BOLD

Boldness is a tough skill to master. But regardless of where you are, what your role is or the size of the workplace, as the leader, when you make bold decisions you have to know that the buck stops with you. Hear everyone out, but you get to make the final decision. I interviewed some employees of a leader recently. And I asked them, 'What are you most excited about being at your organisation?'

And they said, 'The fact that you're talking to us.'

I was confused, 'What do you mean?'

They said the fact that their leader let me come in and talk to them sent them a really strong message about where he was taking the company. I was asking about the company and the vision, but his choice to bring me in was enough for his people to sit up and take notice of his leadership. People want to know that their leader is brave enough to open things up, be challenged and learn. It's inspiring.

However, being bold is not about being frivolous, making big decisions or changing something just for the sake of it. It's what I find the most frustrating: when people go on courses, get coached and come back and make changes just because they've been told to. They've been told it's a good idea, but they haven't understood the context of what's actually needed within their situation.

Be bold, but don't be stupid with it.

STEP 1. **BE BALANCED WITH YOUR BOLDNESS. CHALLENGE AND ENERGISE THE PEOPLE YOU LEAD, BUT DON'T GO AS FAR AS TO DISTRACT OR UPSET PEOPLE.**

STEP 2. **MAKE SURE IT'S THE RIGHT THING TO DO FOR YOUR BUSINESS. THINK ABOUT THE CONTEXT AND MAKE SURE YOUR BOLDNESS DOESN'T END UP DESTROYING WHAT YOU'RE WORKING FOR, OR PUTTING PEOPLE'S JOBS IN DANGER.**

STEP 3. **BEING BOLD STILL MEANS BEING ADAPTABLE AND FLEXIBLE. IF IT'S THE WRONG TIME FOR BOLDNESS, DON'T DO IT JUST FOR THE SAKE OF IT.**

5. FLEXIBILITY

I have a contact who runs an online education business which supplies courses and, occasionally, consultancy. During the pandemic, she assumed everyone would buy her courses because that's where the world was going; everyone had gone online to buy everything. But despite huge marketing efforts it just didn't happen. What did happen was she got a lot of demand for consultancy instead. She went from selling hundreds of courses a year, to five or six clients paying her to go in and tailor the training for them. This was a big change in terms of the vision she had for her business, but she was flexible enough to know this was what she had to do: change her business or close.

Assume there is a solution for every problem and you'll have the ability to discover and implement it, but you have to be flexible. Open yourself up to new ideas and new ways of thinking. You'll not only find a solution, you'll inspire and motivate the people around you, too.

Try 'Brain Steering', a technique from former McKinsey consultants Kevin and Shawn Coyne. Rather than think about how your organisation would cut costs, for example, you'd say, 'Well, if Apple were running our business, how would we cut costs?' or 'If we were Patagonia, how would we treat our staff?' Sometimes you can get so stuck in the ways you've always done things, it can be difficult to be innovative. But if you start thinking about it in unusual ways, asking unexpected questions, removing the emotion, you will find solutions you never thought possible.

THERE WILL ALWAYS BE UNFORESEEN CHALLENGES OR EVENTS YOU HAVE TO FACE AS A LEADER. BE COMMITTED ENOUGH TO STICK TO YOUR VISION OR TARGET BUT BE OPEN TO TAKING DIFFERENT PATHS TO GET THERE. IF YOU'RE NOT GETTING RESULTS, FIND OUT WHY AND THEN TRY A DIFFERENT APPROACH.

“

THERE IS NOTHING LIKE A CONCRETE LIFE PLAN TO WEIGH YOU DOWN. Because if you always have one eye on some future goal, you stop paying attention to the job at hand, miss opportunities that might arise, and stay fixedly on one path, even when a better, newer course might have opened up.

—Indra Nooyi, former CEO at Pepsico

PURPOSE

PURPOSE

1. WE ALL NEED A PURPOSE

Like the waiter who loves to put good food on your table, or the supermarket checkout operator who loves to chat with the regular customers, we all need a sense of purpose. Knowing your purpose is incredibly important on a personal and professional level, and if you can get them both aligned it's brilliant. But don't mistake it for just having an emotional attachment to your work.

Jennifer is the CEO of a charity, but she's not enjoying it. There's a lot of challenges coming from all directions. So, in one of our sessions I asked her the tough question: 'Why don't you leave? What keeps you here?' And she said it was the charity's purpose. Her charity helps inner-city kids take much-needed breaks in the countryside. That's what drives her; she actually gets to see the impact of her work. When she's there, she knows for sure she's helping, unlike other charities where you might not see the impact you make. At that point, the purpose outweighed the stress of everything else. Later, Jennifer did leave that charity after realising that its purpose wasn't enough; she needed something different to feel fulfilled and purposeful. She now works for a different cause where she can make an even greater impact.

When you know your purpose you can overcome those day-to-day challenges and find the positives when it gets tough. People are drawn to, and want to be like, leaders with purpose because they are the ones who will deliver progress and change despite their challenges.

But what if you don't work in such a rewarding environment? Everyone's purpose is unique and it's not always going to match the purpose of your workplace.

Think about it like this:

- What would the world lose if you, or the work you did, disappeared?
- What is your core reason for waking up and making an impact?

I realised late in my corporate career that I'd made my *personal* purpose to make my *company* more successful. Like many people, I didn't have time to think about what my true personal purpose was and it was easier to have it match my company's. But since setting up my consultancy I've realised it's about helping people become better leaders. When a client tells me they thought of my advice when they were in a tough situation, or when I can see the impact of my listening to a senior leader who has no one else to talk to, that's what fulfils me.

When you find your purpose, you can achieve more. It's an enthusiasm and passion that lights up the people around you. It's more than a mission statement, it's the way you connect to your work so you can create value that people need.

STEP 1. **ASK YOURSELF: WHAT'S YOUR PURPOSE? WHAT GETS YOU OUT OF BED EVERY MORNING?**

STEP 2. **IF YOU DON'T KNOW, ASK OTHERS TO TELL YOU WHEN THEY'VE SEEN YOU AT YOUR HAPPIEST, MOST INSPIRED OR MOST FULFILLED.**

STEP 3. **WHEN YOU FIND IT, LET IT BE YOUR GUIDING STAR. EVERY DECISION YOU MAKE, EVERY CLIENT YOU TAKE ON, EVERY PERSON YOU HIRE, MUST POINT IN THE DIRECTION OF YOUR GUIDING STAR.**

2. DON'T LOSE YOUR SPARK

So often when you start your business or take on a leadership role, a lot of it feels very exciting. It's instinctive. It's very much 'this feels right, it's what I want to do'. And because of that, people are drawn to you and follow you. That's why they join your business.

But as time goes on, things change. Maybe the business gets some investors. Suddenly you have advisers. It becomes less about your gut instinct and more about the data or pleasing the board. That's a good thing, and necessary for growth, but for the people in your team it can be a bit less inspiring.

We've all had bosses that only cared about numbers or public perception, and these are important, but most people need more. So don't lose your boldness and your passion. As a leader, you're always 'on'. There is no off-day. Everyone's watching what you're doing, what you're saying and how you're behaving. Everyone is looking to you as a role-model for inspiration to pick them up when things are bad. If they see you're losing your passion and the spark that once inspired them, they're going to start questioning their position, too. Your role as a leader is to make sure you are continuously inspiring and motivating your team towards the shared vision for the company.

EVERYONE NEEDS A PURPOSE. ASIDE FROM MAKING THE BUSINESS MORE PROFIT AND MAKING PEOPLE MORE MONEY, WHAT ARE YOU *REALLY* GOING TO DO? WHAT'S THE VISION? WHERE'S THAT SPARK? ASK YOURSELF WHAT IS DRIVING YOUR DECISION-MAKING RIGHT NOW. IS IT YOUR GUT INSTINCT OR DATA, OR A MIX OF BOTH? SEE WHERE IT LEADS YOU.

"

IF YOU FEEL LIKE THERE'S SOMETHING OUT THERE THAT YOU'RE SUPPOSED TO BE DOING, if you have a passion for it, then stop wishing and just do it.

—Wanda Sykes, American comedian, writer and actor

3. MOMENTS

As you get older it feels like you do fewer 'new' things. You may have fewer exciting experiences and you feel like time really does fly. So, you have to consciously create more new experiences, more things you've never done before. It could be a hobby, a new place or an experience. It could be meeting new people or building new skills. While that won't slow down time, it will make it more measurable.

At the end of each year, I write out everything I did that was different and new. So this year it'll be this book: something I've never done before. Finding those moments is important for you and your team – especially when times are tough and you feel like your team is losing their passion. Creating big moments can reinvigorate and inspire.

One year my team and I had an amazing year. The normal thing to do would have been to go out and celebrate, but instead I decided to spend the budget differently. iPads had just come out, so I thought that if I bought one for each of my team, they would remember they got their first iPad for achieving what they achieved – it turned out to be a really impactful moment.

Here's another one: back in the day when corporate events were really common, someone suggested we do a Spy Training course. My initial reaction was, 'Ah, it's a real hassle, it's miles out of London,' and I had a lot of people who didn't want to do it. The perception was, 'Oh, it'll be a physical thing,' and not everybody wants to do physical things.

But it ended up being a mix of physical and mental challenges. As a team exercise it was the best thing we did because everyone had a role to play at some point. You had people who were amazing at codes, others who were great at puzzles, people who were good at physical challenges, and people who enjoyed team challenges. Almost ten years later I still meet people who left the organisation and talk about Spy Training.

My point is, sometimes it's worth creating these big moments because it sticks in people's minds. People like to work in places where 'things happen'. And that doesn't just apply at work, it also applies in your personal life; if you try and do different things, everything won't just blur into one as you get older. You'll have moments to remember.

STEP 1. **CREATE MOMENTS THAT STICK IN PEOPLE'S MINDS. PEOPLE LIKE TO WORK IN PLACES WHERE THINGS HAPPEN.**

STEP 2. **THE SOLUTION DOESN'T HAVE TO COME FROM YOU; YOU CAN INVITE INSPIRATIONAL PEOPLE IN TO SPEAK OR SHARE POSITIVE FEEDBACK FROM CLIENTS.**

STEP 3. **THINK ABOUT THE INDIVIDUALS IN YOUR TEAM AND HOW YOU CAN CREATE MOMENTS THAT WILL SPEAK TO ALL OF THEM IN DIFFERENT WAYS. IF YOU'RE UNSURE WHAT WILL WORK BEST THEN ASK THEM.**

“

How to balance
PASSION VS. PROFIT.

4. PASSION VS. PROFIT

One day Katy's staff gave her an ultimatum. They told her she needed to fire a client, an oil company, because they felt the client didn't fit their company's values or align with its purpose. So, like any REAL. leader, she listened to their concerns and took time to think about what they said.

People today are looking for a deeper meaning to what they're doing. It means people are choosy about where they work, and where they want to go. And they will leave if it doesn't feel right. It's why (at the time of writing) there is a 'Great Resignation'. One of the biggest challenges leaders are dealing with right now is that people are much more willing to question their organisation's purpose and challenge it.

Katy went back to her team, and was honest, 'Yes, I can fire them,' she admitted, 'but unfortunately, it means I would have to fire you, too. They are one of our biggest clients. At the end of the day, yes, we're here to try and do good things. But at the same time, we've got to run a business and pay wages.' Maybe in the future they can let that client go, but right now it's not possible. It's tough, and as a leader you've got to find that balance between purpose and profit.

Part of being a good leader is being up front with your team. You might have to communicate things you wouldn't normally talk about, or sometimes share a little bit more about the inner workings of the machine. If your team is pushing back and questioning you, it might be because they don't understand what's happening behind the scenes. Have a conversation, and say, 'Yes, this is where we're aiming. We'd love to be able to do this and we'd love to have these great clients but the reality is we also need to keep the office going, keep the lights on, and get everybody paid. We are gradually going to get there. But it's going to take time.'

Everyone has their own purpose for coming to work, but there will be times people will have to make compromises. Stop and think: What's the cost of doing that thing? Will it stop you from doing something else even more amazing that might come along? Will you learn anything from it? Will you be proud of it?

Communicate honestly. People will respect you for it, and it will help them understand *why* you're making the decisions the way you are. And you never know, they may even find ways of solving that problem for you.

STEP 1. **KNOW WHAT YOUR PERSONAL VALUES ARE AS A LEADER. HOW ARE THEY COMMUNICATED AT WORK? DOES EVERYONE IN YOUR TEAM KNOW WHAT THEY ARE?**

STEP 2. **THINK ABOUT YOUR VALUES EVERY TIME YOU TAKE ON A CLIENT, HIRE A NEW RECRUIT OR WORK WITH A NEW SUPPLIER. DO THEY ALIGN?**

STEP 3. **HAVE YOU EVER COMPROMISED ON YOUR VALUES (OR YOUR PASSION) IN ORDER TO MAKE A PROFIT AND, IF SO, HOW DO YOU FEEL ABOUT IT? WHAT COULD YOU DO NEXT TIME?**

5. LIVING THE VISION

To get results, everyone has to have a vision of what they're aiming for. And it's got to be compelling enough that everyone wants to pull together to achieve it. It's got to be exciting, something almost unattainable – and as a leader you've got to paint that picture for your team. It's different from a mission, which is more quantifiable. For example, a vision could be: I want to change the face of leadership forever. Whereas the mission might be: I am going to coach emerging leaders, challenge existing leaders and inspire tomorrow's leaders.

Imagine working for a company that suddenly realised after ten years, it didn't have a clear vision. So, the senior team sits down and decides for everyone, 'Right, this is what we are, this is where we want to go.' And then they go tell the rest of the company. I can guarantee you it will flop. It will flop because it doesn't engage everyone in the organisation, it doesn't connect with them or they feel they have no part in it. Think of it as that guiding star. Once you have a vision everyone can agree on and recognise, communicate it consistently. Promote it in your workplace, on your website, when you're hiring new people, at social events – everywhere. It's got to be a vision everyone is living every day. Check in with your clients and teams regularly. Is everyone on the same page? Ask them, 'Are we staying true to this? Does it need any course correction? Do we need more training?'

A vision is not about saying, 'This is what we're doing,' and dragging people with you. It's about asking people, 'How do you think we can achieve this together?' A vision adapts over time and reacts to all kinds of external influences. And most importantly, it belongs to everyone. You mustn't look like you have all the answers when you're creating your vision, even if you feel like you do.

STEP 1. START WITH PAINTING A PICTURE OF YOUR VISION. COMMUNICATE IT TO YOUR TEAM AND MAKE SURE THAT YOU INVOLVE THEM.

STEP 2. BE READY TO ADAPT IT AS YOU GO SO THAT YOU ALWAYS STICK TO THAT VISION. IT NEEDS TO UNDERPIN EVERYTHING YOU DO.

STEP 3. KEEP CHECKING IN. DOES IT STILL RESONATE WITH STAFF? IS IT CLEAR TO THOSE OUTSIDE YOUR WORKPLACE? DOES IT NEED CHANGING?

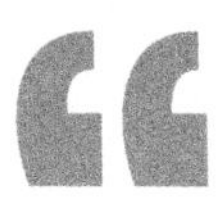

IF YOU THINK YOU'RE LEADING AND NO ONE IS FOLLOWING YOU, then you're only taking a walk.

—Afghan proverb

RESULTS

COMMUNICATION

COMMUNICATION

1. EFFECTIVE COMMUNICATION

If you look at why people join, stay at or leave organisations, it's because they want to feel connected. We all want leaders and organisations we can believe in, champion and understand. Therefore, leaders must give people what they need, when they need it. And one of those is *effective* communication.

Look at all the great communicators you admire, they work hard on their communication skills. They prepare what they're going to say and how they're going to say it. They think about their audience and they test their message. You can never do enough preparation in terms of communication. A leader's words and actions can help people feel connected, supported emotionally and put their experience into a context where they can draw meaning from it.

You have to understand how essential this skill is, and you must look at ways you can improve it. Even if you're confident and you know you're a great communicator, always talk to your team to be sure. Are there ways you could be better?

Mickela Hall-Ramsay says, 'Know who you're working with. Our apprentice: I know that speaking to him and expecting him to write down notes is not going to work. He will probably attempt 10% of whatever I ask him. Whereas if I email him, it will be better because it will be in writing. But I know the best way for him is to communicate using WhatsApp voice notes, so he can easily play it. He won't read it wrong and he's able to fulfil the task better. Whereas another person will prefer having the email because it's visual. Someone else will prefer to see me face to face. So again, it's about knowing who you're working with.'

Find out what the best communication style is for your team because, as a leader, you need to communicate in the best way for them. Remember, you don't get to choose how you communicate with them, they do.

STEP 1. COMMUNICATE CLEARLY AND FREQUENTLY. MAINTAIN TRANSPARENCY AND HELP PEOPLE MAKE SENSE OF ALL THAT HAS HAPPENED.

STEP 2. ASK YOUR TEAM WHAT COMMUNICATION STYLE WOULD BE BEST FOR THEM.

STEP 3. IF YOU HAVE FEARS OR WEAKNESSES AROUND COMMUNICATION, THAT'S A SIGN TO WORK ON THOSE AREAS.

2. CHAMELEON LEADERSHIP[2]

When you lead, you need to make decisions and get results. And to do that you need to have people around you that are going to support your choices. If you haven't built those kinds of relationships – if you don't have allies – it's going to be

2 Chameleon Leadership: https://hbr.org/2007/11/eight-ways-to-build-collaborative-teams

really, really tough. Traditional leaders were probably brought up to show everyone they were bulletproof. To dominate, rule and communicate in a way that demanded people adapted and bent to their will. But that doesn't work anymore. To build a strong relationship with allies and supporters you have to adapt the way you communicate with different people, while still being authentic and empathetic (skills we'll talk about in the next part of the book). This style of leadership is about meeting people where they are, rather than expecting them to come to you.

In a study of 55 teams within 15 multinational companies[3] it was found that the most productive and innovative workplaces had leaders who could switch their skills as needed. They could be task- or relationship-oriented depending on the stage of their project or the needs of the team. At the early stages they were task-oriented, making the goal clear and clarifying team member responsibilities. Later on they would switch to building relationships and focus on building the team. Marc Convey (one of our Everyday Leaders) agrees that, 'as a leader you have to wear different hats, so there's a lot of pressure on you to have those various different character traits'. One of the toughest skills leaders learn is how to stay authentic and consistent while adapting and communicating with different people. It means using certain skills more in some situations, and less in others – and knowing when to change that up with each situation.

3 Eight Ways to Build Collaborative Teams (hbr.org)

ADAPT YOUR COMMUNICATION DEPENDING ON WHO YOU TALK TO. IT'S ALL ABOUT SITUATIONAL AND CONTEXTUAL AWARENESS. HOW DOES IT CHANGE WHEN YOU ARE TASK-ORIENTED VS. WHEN YOU ARE RELATIONSHIP-ORIENTED? HOW WILL YOU ADAPT YOUR COMMUNICATION WHEN YOU'RE TALKING TO YOUR TEAM, YOUR PEERS OR YOUR SUPERIORS?

3. LEADING WITH WORDS

A key part of being a leader is leading by example. Don't expect people to do anything you wouldn't do yourself. Inspire from being out in front and showing your team you understand the challenges of what they're going through. You don't have to be the best person in the role, but you do have to have an understanding and empathy for what the role entails.

But what if you don't understand what they're going through? What if you've inherited a team, or been given a leadership role you feel unsuited to? Firstly, it's about communicating and setting the tone from the first time you meet. Once, I had to relocate to America and I inherited the HR team. I knew nothing about HR, my experience was in sales. So the first thing I did was sit everyone down and be honest. I told them, 'I've been put in this role because I know the business inside out, I can get things done. But now I need to find out how that applies to HR. I don't have all the answers and I'm not going to teach you how to do your job. But I will teach you how to succeed in this organisation, how to get credit for what you achieve and how to be proud of your work.'

I ran a a number of half-day workshop so I could learn and understand everything they did. I listened to everything they wanted and made sure *they* understood what *I* could bring to the team.

Leading from the front means thinking about your team, what they need from you and how you can help them achieve it. As you become more senior, you'll see it becomes more about their success than yours.

Another client, Nina, struggled with celebrating with her team. Not because they weren't brilliant, but because she wanted to be humble. She didn't want to show off. I had to remind her that when you report back and present the work you've done, it's not about you, it's about your team. It's about telling everyone how great your team is. It's important that you represent them, wave the flag for them and shout about them from the rooftops. Because they'll be expecting you to be an advocate for them. That's part of your job as their leader.

STEP 1. **AS A LEADER YOU'RE ALWAYS 'ON' AND LEADING BY EXAMPLE; YOU CAN'T TURN IT ON AND OFF. THAT'S THE CHALLENGE OF REAL, AUTHENTIC LEADERSHIP.**

STEP 2. **IT'S NOT ALWAYS ABOUT HOW YOU LEAD, IT'S ABOUT HOW OTHERS EXPERIENCE YOUR LEADERSHIP. IT'S NOT ABOUT YOUR EGO, IT'S ABOUT REPRESENTING YOUR TEAM'S ACHIEVEMENTS AND SUCCESSES AT EVERY TURN.**

STEP 3. YOU DON'T HAVE TO BE THE CLEVEREST OR MOST EXPERIENCED IN YOUR TEAM. A REAL. LEADER SURROUNDS THEMSELVES WITH PEOPLE WHO ARE BEST AT THEIR SPECIFIC ROLES.

"

LEADERSHIP IS MORE THAN JUST BEING IN CHARGE – it's inspiring, collaborating, and working with others towards a bigger cause.

—Ronald Reagan

4. SWITCHING OFF

When I was working in a corporate role, for probably the first 15 years of my career I always took my phone with me on holiday. I was always checking emails and working. Then one year, my wife booked a place with no reception. No wi-fi. I remember getting to this place and I was mortified when I found out that I couldn't use my phone. She said, 'That's the whole point. There's no wi-fi so you have to switch off.' My reaction was to storm off to the nearest village and find wi-fi so I could tell everyone why they couldn't get hold of me. But once I'd got over my strop, it was the best holiday ever. After that it became our thing; I never took my phone away on holiday. If someone needed to get hold of me, they had the number of where we were staying but that's it.

There was never a situation that was so bad I had to stop my holiday for work. And it was amazing to see how many times people were able to sort stuff out on their own. I didn't actually need to be a part of that decision.

The lesson here is this: the success of your organisation is based on you – not being *physically* the one to fix everything, but *helping* other people to be like you, grow like you and learn how to lead for themselves. If you can show you trust your team to look after themselves, you'll reap the rewards.

Leaders now are dealing with so many more emotional factors than they were in the past. And it's a drain on you. Taking time off is important for your mental well-being, and perhaps we hadn't realised that before. And I can guarantee you the benefits of doing this will cascade down through your team. It's leading by example, giving your team permission to switch off.

STEP 1. UNDERSTAND THAT YOU NEED TIME OFF AND THAT IT'S IMPORTANT.

STEP 2. DON'T AGONISE OVER WHAT TIME OFF LOOKS LIKE. IF YOU WANT TO TAKE A WEDNESDAY OFF THAT'S FINE. IF YOU WANT TO TAKE A WEEK OFF THAT'S OK, TOO.

STEP 3. IF YOU FEEL LIKE YOU CAN'T SWITCH OFF, ASK YOURSELF, WHY? IS THERE A CULTURE OF PRESENTEEISM? DO YOU FEEL UNSUPPORTED? FIND OUT WHAT'S GOING ON AND TRY TO FIND A SOLUTION THAT ALLOWS YOU TIME TO SWITCH OFF.

5. PUBLIC SPEAKING

One of the biggest fears people have when it comes to communication is public speaking. Because when you're standing up as a leader, you know you could get tough questions. You're the face of the organisation. It's you on the line.

If I knew I had to do some public speaking the following day, I wouldn't be able to sleep until I'd gone through my whole presentation three times without any mistakes. In my mind, if I could do it three times with no mistakes, it would be good. But that meant I often wouldn't go to bed until 2am or 3am and I'd be exhausted the next day.

But when you communicate, it's not because you're fulfilling some selfish need. It's not about you, it's for the people listening to you. That's why it irritates me so much when people don't care enough to develop good communication skills. If you don't care how you come across, how people see you or hear you, it means you don't care about the people you're talking to.

The best training I ever had was from a public speaking specialist, and it involved improvisational comedy. His job was to make us more confident, so if we were ever pulled up in front of the press, or had to give a comment, we would know what to say. At the end of two days of training we could talk about anything without any preparation. We learned that if you're calm and just be yourself, your brain will do the work; even if you find the most tenuous link somewhere, you can still talk to people about anything and it will be entertaining.

When you're communicating publicly, make sure you connect with your audience – with humour, with emotion or whatever it is they need from you. The world has changed. People don't expect leaders to be bulletproof or to be amazing presenters, they just want someone they can connect with.

STEP 1. **YOU DON'T HAVE TO BE THE BEST PRESENTER, EVERY TIME. ABOVE ANYTHING ELSE YOUR TEAM WILL BE LOOKING FOR HONESTY, SINCERITY AND AUTHENTICITY. BEING ENTERTAINING OR INSPIRATIONAL HELPS, BUT IT'S NOT ESSENTIAL.**

STEP 2. **IF YOU HAVE TIME TO PREPARE THEN DO IT. ROLEPLAY YOUR PRESENTATION AND CHECK IT WITH OTHERS TO GET CONSTRUCTIVE FEEDBACK.**

STEP 3. **THINK OF THIS PLANE ANALOGY: WHEN YOU START YOU'RE TAKING EVERYONE ON A JOURNEY, THEY ARE EXCITED AND ENGAGED. BUT THEY'LL SOON GET SLEEPY OR BORED AND WILL WANT TO GET OFF. STOP 'CIRCLING AIMLESSLY' AND ENSURE YOUR CONTENT IS INTERESTING. FINALLY, 'LAND THE PLANE'. IN OTHER WORDS, LAND YOUR MAIN MESSAGE, ROUND OFF THE PRESENTATION AND REMIND YOUR AUDIENCE OF WHERE YOU WERE WHEN YOU STARTED THE JOURNEY.**

6. OVER-COMMUNICATING

Even when you think you've communicated well, how can you be sure your message actually got across? I'd always be surprised by how I could say something in a meeting in the morning, but when I followed up in the afternoon people would say, 'Oh, was that what you meant? I didn't get that.'

By over-communication I mean it's on you to make sure people understand your message. When you communicate something, you've got to check in with them, and you've got to say it again. Keep going until you know for sure it's been heard in the way you intended, and understood. You'll be surprised by how many people miss something simply because they've got their own issues to deal with. Don't forget that working remotely has made us overly sensitive to unexpected or slow responses. This happens professionally and personally, and I spend a lot of time telling clients, friends and family not to overreact. Understand that people have their own stuff going on and you're not always the priority.

To help, you'll need people around you who are honest and can challenge you if what you say doesn't sound right. You need people who can tell you after you've miscommunicated that you did it wrong. And you've got to be able to take what they say on board and rectify it. When you communicate you need to check in again, and again, and again.

Imagine you announce a new vision for your workplace. But when you speak to people about it, they get it wrong or they don't understand it. When that happens it's not their fault, it's yours. Because it hadn't been communicated in a way that resonated with them.

So when you check in with people, create a safe space

for them to tell you if your communications are, or aren't, working. For example, when one of my clients updated his company's vision and mission, he liked to stop his staff randomly and ask them if they'd heard and understood it. He'd say, 'Hi, can you tell me what the vision is? And if you can't, don't worry about it, it means that I haven't done my job.' If they didn't know or didn't understand it, it was on him. When I first work with people, I like to say, 'Call me out if I'm talking bullshit.' If I get something wrong, I say sorry and rectify it.

As a leader you have to create a space where over-communication is normal, but not patronising. Don't assume you need to follow up with everyone, it's about creating a space where people can be honest with you and comfortable enough to say, 'I didn't get that, can you explain it again?'

STEP 1. **CHECK IN REGULARLY WITH PEOPLE TO MAKE SURE THEY UNDERSTAND YOUR MESSAGE.**

STEP 2. **IF THEY DON'T UNDERSTAND, OR DON'T KNOW WHAT YOU'VE COMMUNICATED, YOU NEED TO TAKE RESPONSIBILITY AND FIX IT.**

STEP 3. **CREATE A SAFE SPACE FOR PEOPLE TO TELL YOU WHEN YOU GET IT WRONG, OR FOR THEM TO QUESTION YOU.**

7. HONESTY

People follow authentic and honest leaders, so your communication needs to be the same. I don't think you should ever stand up and say, 'Listen, I'm not quite sure what's going on here. Things aren't looking good.' But it's about saying, 'OK, I might not know what's going on, but here's what I'm going to do to find out.' You decide to set up a committee, or talk to an expert. You're going to spend the next two days going over the data. You're going to create an Ideas Box and you want people to come to you with fresh ideas.

If things aren't going well, there's no point in giving people a PowerPoint on it. Tell them what you're going to do to improve things. What's the plan? And if you don't know, don't be afraid to say, 'I need help making a plan.' Ask the best brains on your team to help you. Get people in. You've got to instil a feeling of moving forward all the time. Don't be paralysed by problems. 'You don't have to know everything when you're a leader. You honestly don't,' maintains Dr. Eunice Ndirangu-Mugo. 'But make sure you tell people how you're going to find the knowledge and get things fixed.'

STEP 1. IF THE SITUATION IS BAD, THEN FRONT IT UP AND LET EVERYONE KNOW WHAT YOU'RE DOING ABOUT IT. YOU'RE NOT GUARANTEEING IT WILL WORK OR THINGS WILL IMPROVE, BUT YOU'RE REASSURING THEM YOU'RE DOING SOMETHING ABOUT IT.

STEP 2. IF YOU HAVE GOOD NEWS THEN MAKE SURE YOU CONGRATULATE THE PEOPLE WHO MADE IT HAPPEN AND GIVE CREDIT AND RECOGNITION WHERE IT'S DUE. MAKE A CHECKLIST OR ASK A COLLEAGUE TO HELP YOU REMEMBER WHO TO THANK!

STEP 3. IF YOU'RE WORRIED ABOUT HOW THE NEWS WILL BE TAKEN, ROLEPLAY WITH SOME OF THE ATTENDEES TO TEST OUT THE MESSAGE BEFOREHAND.

"

WHEN SENIOR PEOPLE GIVE OPAQUE ANSWERS, IT'S ONE OF THE MOST UNTRUSTWORTHY THINGS THEY CAN DO … I find that people who share ambiguity when situations are tough to call are far more impressive.

—Martha Lane Fox, co-founder of Lastminute.com and Lucky Voice

8. RECOGNITION IS PERSONAL, NOT PROGRAMMATIC

In 2016, a US-focused Gallup survey discovered that staff who didn't feel recognised for their achievements were twice as likely to say they'd quit the following year. The solution? Give praise and regular feedback frequently.

But a robotic system of reward won't work. If you've got a team that knows if they perform well every month, they get to go out for dinner and drinks, it stops being a 'reward'. Tailored and personalised rewards are more effective. Everyone has different motivations and priorities. If you reward someone with one extra day off, to some people that may not be what works for them. If you have a big team with lots of different demographics you may think dinner and late-night drinks is a good idea, but what about all the parents? That might be the worst reward. Equally, if you take people out on a speedboat on the Thames, what about people who don't find that fun – is that really going to be a reward? You've got to cater for all these different needs.

You could argue that coming to work and being paid is enough recognition, but I think everyone craves something more. And it doesn't have to be a big thing; it can be as simple as a 'thank you' or an unexpected gesture. Maybe instead of a free iPad or vouchers for a meal say, 'I saw what you did and I appreciate it.' A casual conversation here or there, or a simple action like buying someone their favourite coffee, could mean the world to one of your colleagues or clients.

Be creative with rewards, too; I used to sometimes take people for a quick breakfast in the morning. I'm not saying that buying someone a meal, or saying 'thanks' is the answer, but it's important to make it personal and find out for sure what will mean the most to that person.

Everyday defining moments bring opportunities to have conversations that leave you or the other person changed in some way. And if you don't know what rewards are best, find out. I used to spend a lot of time discussing this with my team. Ask the people you work with: 'So what motivates Alex, you know them better than I do?' or, 'What would be a great thing to say to Aaron?' or, 'What's the best way to thank Hannah?'

STEP 1. **TALK TO PEOPLE. IF THERE'S SOMEONE ON YOUR TEAM YOU DON'T KNOW VERY WELL, ASK SOMEONE WHO IS CLOSE TO THEM. FIND OUT WHAT WOULD MEAN THE MOST TO THEM.**

STEP 2. **DO A BIT OF RESEARCH AND BE AWARE OF YOUR TEAM AND WHAT MOTIVATES THEM. ARE BIG TEAM EVENTS REALLY WHAT THEY WANT, OR DO THEY TEND TO FAVOUR SMALLER EXPERIENCES? DO THEY WANT MATERIAL THINGS OR EXPERIENCES?**

STEP 3. **BE POSITIVE AND SINCERE. DON'T SHOW APPRECIATION BECAUSE I TOLD YOU TO AND IT TICKS A BOX. DO IT BECAUSE YOU WANT TO AND THEY DESERVE IT.**

EMPATHY

“

BE DECENT TO PEOPLE. TREAT EVERYONE WITH FAIRNESS AND EMPATHY. THIS DOESN'T MEAN THAT YOU LOWER YOUR EXPECTATIONS OR CONVEY THE MESSAGE THAT MISTAKES DON'T MATTER. It means that you create an environment where people know you'll hear them out, that you're emotionally consistent and fair-minded.

—Robert Iger

EMPATHY

1. DO YOU REALLY CARE?

Before the pandemic, empathy was seen as a weak leadership skill. Now, it's a strength. The best leaders don't have to try and be empathetic, they just are. And if you aren't, you've got no chance as a leader these days.

Embedding empathy into an organisation needs to come from the top. As a leader you must make it clear that people come first and understanding different perspectives is not only important internally, but also good for business; for example, being able to understand what a client wants by putting yourself in their shoes will lead to better work.

When Marc Convey was first setting up 23D he quickly realised that while he'd become the leader off the back of his knowledge and expertise, his leadership needed to evolve; he needed to be a more approachable and empathetic leader, too. Previously, as a freelancer, he'd discovered that the key to his success was understanding people and giving them what they want. He knew that while results are a short-term gain, success comes from empathy, care and building those long-term relationships.

However, despite caring, some people do struggle to show empathy. One of my clients, Ben, finds it hard. We've spent a lot of time talking about how he can demonstrate it in his working day: asking how people are at the start of a meeting, allowing time for a quick social chat or doing impromptu check-ins with staff. We've even discussed keeping a calendar or diary about conversations he's had so he can follow up with someone who mentioned they'd had a tough weekend.

It doesn't matter whether it comes naturally to you or not, it doesn't matter *how* you show empathy – people want to know their leaders take an interest and they care.

STEP 1. **MAKE DEMONSTRATING EMPATHY PART OF YOUR DAILY ROUTINE. IF YOU ASK HOW SOMEONE IS, BE IN THE MOMENT AND REALLY CARE ABOUT THE ANSWER. IF YOU THINK THAT SOMETHING IS TROUBLING THEM, THEN ASK HOW THEY ARE AGAIN. YOU'LL BE SURPRISED HOW MANY PEOPLE OPEN UP WHEN YOU ASK THEM A SECOND TIME.**

STEP 2. **IF YOU STRUGGLE TO SHOW EMPATHY, BUILD EMPATHY ACTIONS AND TASKS INTO YOUR DAY SO IT BECOMES A HABIT. IT MAY FEEL FAKE AT FIRST BUT EVENTUALLY IT WILL BECOME SECOND NATURE.**

STEP 3. **GET SOMEONE TO HELP YOU. CREATE A ROLE LIKE 'CHIEF OF STAFF' OR 'EMPLOYEE HAPPINESS MANAGER'. IF YOUR SECOND-IN-COMMAND IS BETTER AT SHOWING EMPATHY, ASK THEM TO TAKE THIS ON AND REPORT BACK TO YOU SO YOU STILL UNDERSTAND AND CARE FOR YOUR STAFF.**

2. THE PERSON IN FRONT OF YOU

My brother once worked as a hotel porter and was told that Bill Clinton was going to turn up at his hotel. The staff had to stand out at reception to welcome him when he arrived and, as a porter, my brother was put at the end of the line; obviously considered not one of the important people.

When the 42nd president of the United States turned up, instead of brushing past the staff and disappearing inside the hotel, he made a point of talking to everybody in the line. When he got to my brother, he stopped and they had a conversation: What was his background? Why was he at this hotel? My brother knew that the hotel manager was absolutely panicking at this point, but he didn't care. At that moment, my brother felt like the most important person in the world.

Obviously, Bill Clinton may have his share of human shortcomings, but as a communicator he was amazing. He could make you feel like you were the most important person there and I think this is a really great leadership skill to have. This is how you want to make people feel. People come first and the person standing in front of you is the most important, no matter who they are. Another good example of this was Queen Elizabeth II. During her funeral it became clear what a lasting impact she had made on people, simply by them sharing a few words with her or shaking her hand. Someone described them as 'micro-moments'.

Use this with your team. They need to know you really care, and the person you are talking to, no matter what their role, is as important as everybody else. It means dealing with issues that might seem small to you but are huge to them.

Your workplace will only be as successful as the team of people you have following you.

BUILD IN TIME TO TALK TO YOUR PEOPLE, SO YOU CAN DEVELOP THOSE RELATIONSHIPS. YOU'RE NEVER TOO IMPORTANT TO HAVE A QUICK CONVERSATION OR TO HELP STAFF WITH A PROBLEM. THAT MEANS HONOURING CATCH-UP MEETINGS AND CHECK-INS. DON'T RE-PRIORITISE THEM OR REARRANGE, THEY ARE AS IMPORTANT AS YOUR BIG MEETINGS. BUILD A CULTURE THAT PRIORITISES ITS PEOPLE.

3. THE THREE TYPES OF EMOTIONAL INTELLIGENCE

According to psychologists Daniel Goleman and Paul Ekman[4] there are three kinds of empathy that reside in the brain:

Cognitive: *I know what you think*
Emotional: *I know how you feel*
Empathetic Concern: *I care about you*

Most people have the first two. When you speak to a colleague in the morning, and they say, 'I've had a terrible night', or 'my dog's ill,' you can empathise. You can understand their situation and perhaps feel what they are going through.

4 https://www.youtube.com/watch?v=9oQxFUo9zfM&t=41s

The third one is where you care but actually want to *do something about it*. This is the bit most leaders don't have because most leaders, when they've had that first conversation with someone, say, 'Oh, sorry to hear that,' and then move on to the next thing on their list.

If you're a truly empathetic leader and want to show empathetic concern, follow up with that person who's been struggling. You might speak to their line manager and ask them to check in for you. When I worked in an open-plan office with about 150 people I always stopped to ask people how they were. I was notoriously late for every meeting but those unplanned moments led to some immensely valuable conversations.

At Mummy's Star, Pete Wallroth makes it clear to staff that it's OK to take a break during the day, especially if they've had a challenging experience: 'If you've had to do a support call for a family that's in bits,' he tells them, 'go away, get out of the house for a walk, do some yoga, take the dog out, I don't care. Go and do it. Do it in work time. Don't do it later when you finish for the day, do it now.' In doing so, he's created a culture where his team are comfortable enough to show empathetic concern for him in return: 'I've had some of the team pull me up on it, too. They say "Yeah, but are you going out as well?" I'm like, "Yeah, I will do, later." And they say, "Yeah, you're doing it now."' That's the kind of culture of care you want to create.

And this isn't just within your professional life, this is within your personal life as well.

BEING EMPATHETIC CANNOT BE RUSHED OR SCHEDULED. THAT MEANS TAKING YOUR TIME, STAYING IN THE MOMENT AND LISTENING TO THE PERSON. DON'T THINK ABOUT THE NEXT MEETING OR YOUR NEXT TASK, TRULY HEAR WHAT THE PERSON YOU'RE WITH HAS TO SAY. CREATING A CULTURE AROUND EMPATHETIC CONCERN MEANS YOUR ORGANISATION PRIORITISES THE WELL-BEING OF YOUR PEOPLE. IT MEANS YOU ACTUALLY PUT PROCESSES IN PLACE THAT HELP PEOPLE SOLVE THEIR PROBLEMS AND DEMONSTRATE EMPATHY.

PEOPLE

EMPATHY

PEOPLE

1. THE MODERN EMPLOYEE

Working is not just about making money. According to McKinsey today, about two-thirds of millennials take a company's social and environmental commitments into account when deciding where to work.[5] New generations of talent have expectations that challenge previous norms. Practical perks like flexible hours or free breakfasts no longer hold as much value. People want a wider sense of connection and purpose that underpins their working experience. There's a move towards a working style that is emotionally intelligent but also prioritises ethical and sustainable practices.

The key thing here is to truly understand your employees as individuals, whether they're millennials, Gen X, Gen Z or the next generation coming through. For example, Gen Z could be craving more personal relationships because of the social isolation the pandemic placed on our lives. They might be coming through with a sense of resilience, driving sustainability and pushing green movements. So what could that mean for your workplace? How will your leadership help fulfil those motivations?

5 https://www.mckinsey.com/capabilities/people-and-organizational-performance/our-insights/purpose-shifting-from-why-to-how

This is not a box-ticking exercise, it's about embracing what your people are looking for. Know what they want and change the way your organisation works to support that. It's not enough to set up a committee, throw some money at it, stick a few people on it and hit some KPIs for the next few months. You need to look at the world your team was brought up in and now live in – what's their perspective on the world? How can you help them fulfil their purpose?

TAKE TIME TO UNDERSTAND YOUR TEAM. WHAT GENERATION DO THEY BELONG TO AND DOES IT INFORM THEIR NEEDS? DON'T ASSUME THAT BECAUSE THEY BELONG TO A CERTAIN GENERATION, THEY FIT INTO WHATEVER THAT MODEL IS. THIS COMES BACK TO UNDERSTANDING AND MANAGING DIFFERENT PERSONALITIES; SOMETHING THAT HAS ALWAYS BEEN A LEADERSHIP REQUIREMENT. YOU SHOULD SPEND TIME UNDERSTANDING INDIVIDUALS' MOTIVATIONS.

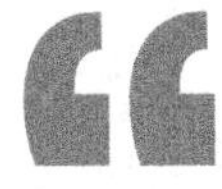

LEADERSHIP IS NOT ABOUT YOU, it's about them.

—Toto Wolff, Team Principal and CEO of Mercedes Formula One Team

2. HYBRID WORKING

The biggest empathy test for leaders is hybrid working. Some companies recruited people during the pandemic who expected certain ways of working; remote working and flexible hours, for example. But now everything is back to 'normal', people are being asked back into the office and they're confused – this wasn't what they signed up for. If leaders think they can get back to what life was like before the pandemic, I think they're going to have a rude awakening. It's why people are leaving jobs and reassessing their entire careers. Bizarrely, you've got other companies that got rid of a lot of their office space to save money, but now people want to go back in; there's now too many people and not enough office space.

As well as empathy, hybrid working comes down to trust. Do you trust your people when they are working from home? If you don't, then there's an issue with you as a leader, or you need to address what your team has done to break your trust and what they need to do to earn it.

James added 20 employees to his organisation during the pandemic. His culture was changing, but he'd never physically met any of these people. He said, 'I know it's wrong, but I'm struggling with trusting them and knowing what they're doing.'

So, I asked him, 'What is actually important in terms of output? What are you actually looking for? Does it matter whether someone can do it in two hours? If they're still giving you the output you want, and they're not missing deadlines, does that work for you?'

I have another client, Richard, who had big plans to implement a four-day week while still paying his staff a full-time wage. He got everyone's opinions and they all came back saying it was a great idea. But he later found out that some of the team were doing other jobs on the fifth day, seeing it as an opportunity to earn extra money. He was furious – he saw it as him paying them to go and earn more money elsewhere. But when he confronted them about it, they said, 'You did this for our well-being, but that fifth day is *our* day. Isn't it up to us what we do with it?' As a leader he didn't know how to react, and I'll be honest it took me some time to think of a solution, too. Eventually he decided to discuss it directly with the team and then individuals. He highlighted why he was frustrated and how important that fifth day was for their well-being and being able to tackle the four days effectively. He also had honest conversations with the few people that were taking extra jobs to understand why they needed to do that and whether he could help.

Hybrid working falls under empathy because there are so many variables. You have to be very understanding and empathetic to what people are going through, but at the same time you have to keep your business running and make sure you've got that social engagement and working culture.

Regardless of how the work is done, the best leaders should be setting clear goals for their teams and making sure they have the tools to achieve that. It shouldn't really matter how or where they hit those goals.

YOU WANT TO DO THE RIGHT THING, BUT THERE IS NO PLAYBOOK AND NO PERFECT SOLUTION. EVERY ORGANISATION IS DIFFERENT AND WILL HAVE DIFFERENT NEEDS, SO FIND WAYS TO CONTINUOUSLY ADAPT. THE DANGEROUS THING TO DO IS TO FIX YOUR DECISIONS IN STONE. KEEP GETTING FEEDBACK AND REVIEWING YOUR HYBRID WORKING PROCESSES. FIND A BALANCE BETWEEN THE NEEDS OF YOUR TEAM AND THE NEEDS OF YOUR ORGANISATION.

3. AUTOCRATIC LEADERSHIP

Any leader who is autocratic means they tend to lead from the top and not listen to their team: 'It's my way or the highway.' They sit in an ivory tower somewhere, aren't empathetic and probably not authentic either. They don't lead by example and expect other people to do the things they wouldn't do themselves. This type of leader refuses to listen to those below who can provide vital feedback and might help avert a crisis. For me that's a traditional view of leadership that we need to change.

This is different from being the type of leader who does what they need to do to get things done. Sometimes there's a place for autocratic decision-making, like during times of emergency or in the military. We saw it during the pandemic, where there wasn't time to set up committees and debate what was best. Action was needed. But I don't think you need to be like this all the time; it's when leaders keep using this style once the problem has passed that it becomes a problem.

Mickela Hall-Ramsay once had a part-time job with a manager that was, in her words, running a dictatorship. Her contract was for eight hours in the evenings as she was still studying at university. And she had a second job. But her manager didn't seem to care, and he would schedule her on the rota to work mornings when she would have been studying at university. He made her time unbearable and she eventually quit, vowing never to lead like him. It made her realise that you need to create a positive environment with the people on your team. You need to work together for the same goal. Perhaps if he'd taken the time to get to know her, he'd realise she was juggling studies and a second job. But he didn't, and he lost an excellent team member.

If you're trying to lead an organisation that's stuck in an autocratic culture, it's important to understand why it's like that and look for opportunities to start a change. Ultimately, it's going to come down to proving your version of leadership is better.

UNDERSTAND WHAT AUTOCRATIC LEADERSHIP IS AND WHEN YOU MIGHT NEED TO USE IT. REMEMBER THERE'S A TIME AND A PLACE FOR IT. KEEP COMMUNICATION OPEN WITH YOUR TEAM AND THE PEOPLE WHO HOLD YOU ACCOUNTABLE. IF YOU FIND YOU'RE BEING AUTOCRATIC, OR AREN'T BRINGING THE TEAM WITH YOU, THEN DO SOMETHING ABOUT IT.

4. GIVING FEEDBACK

If you give feedback using the wrong tone or words, you'll lose the opportunity to truly engage and coach someone. I think a lot of leaders struggle to give negative feedback without demotivating people. They're worried about saying the wrong thing and risking people leaving. So, a lot of leaders push it to the bottom of their list because it can feel as horrible as firing someone. Organisations go to great lengths to create a 'family atmosphere', but I think that's sometimes the worst atmosphere – you don't want to feel like you're telling off your kids or disagreeing with your partner. But giving advice or feedback is just a skill and it's one you can improve. There are certain ways of phrasing things (and I don't mean using the 'Shit Sandwich' method – it's too well known, everyone knows when it's happening to them).

My favourite method is to just be honest. Don't sugar-coat it. For me, if I was giving negative feedback to someone, 90% of the time the reason they'd done something wrong was because I hadn't coached or properly supported them.

I hadn't given them the tools to succeed. Only rarely was it something they had done deliberately.

When giving feedback, time it for when it's most impactful – either the moment the mistake was made or within the day. Doing it later, or when you feel more confident, is not how leaders give feedback.

Christine, a client of mine, had a team member who was particularly vocal, verging on bullying. So, a few hours after the incident, she would gather her thoughts and then tell them what they'd done wrong. But the feedback would never seem to land. The next time this person stepped out of line, Christine immediately pulled them aside (sometimes feedback is all about timing) and told them their behaviour was not acceptable and it landed.

The aim of feedback is to help someone go away feeling like they've learned from it and that they can do something afterwards. Most importantly when you give negative feedback, always follow up. Make sure they understand what you discussed and aren't struggling with any changes you agreed on.

STEP 1. **SEE FEEDBACK AS AN OPPORTUNITY TO ENGAGE AND COACH SOMEONE TO IMPROVE WHAT THEY'RE DOING. DON'T GO IN THINKING YOU'RE GOING TO MAKE THEM FEEL SMALL.**

STEP 2. **GIVE SOMEONE SPACE TO FIND THEIR OWN SOLUTIONS. THERE WILL BE HEIGHTENED EMOTIONS HERE, SO GIVE THEM TIME AND LET THEM FIGURE OUT WHAT TO DO NEXT.**

STEP 3. **TALK THROUGH THE SOLUTION, ONLY OFFERING YOUR VIEW OF WHAT TO DO NEXT IF THEY GIVE YOU PERMISSION.**

STEP 4. **USE THE EIGHT STEPS TO APPROACHING TOUGH CONVERSATION.**

HOW TO APPROACH TOUGH CONVERSATIONS

1. Focus on the goal
– do what's right for them (and your company) not what they want.

2. Get advice if you need it
– legal, HR, coach.

3. Prepare, practice, roleplay.

4. Know your style
– rollover, fight or negotiate.

5. Make your point then listen
– avoid the s**t sandwich approach.

6. Show empathy
– put yourself in their shoes, provide a safe space.

7. Control your anger or defensive impulse
– stick to your goal.

8. Learn from it for next time.

5. THE WISDOM ECONOMY[6]

THE KNOWLEDGE ECONOMY DEMANDS QUALIFICATIONS.

THE WISDOM ECONOMY INSISTS ON QUALITIES FIRST.

IN THE KNOWLEDGE ECONOMY IT'S 'DOG EAT DOG'.

IN THE WISDOM ECONOMY IT'S 'DOGS DO BETTER IN PACKS'.

When I first heard this, it really resonated with me. It's not just about having the skills and technical ability to do something, it's about having the right attitude and will to do it as well. In most roles, you can teach people the technical stuff (unless it's something really tough like brain surgery or law), but what you can't teach is determination or enthusiasm. Think of nurses. Nurses have to get qualifications in order to practise, but it's their empathy and ability to care that will take a good nurse to an exceptional nurse.

The Wisdom Economy prioritises the team over the individual. And it's not just about having a team with the most qualifications, but a team of people with similar values, passions and purpose. 'Loads of people can satisfy a job spec, but not everybody can do a job,' Pete Wallroth says of

6 The Wisdom Economy: https://www.thersa.org/comment/2010/03/from-a-knowledge-economy-to-a-wisdom-economy

recruitment. When you structure a team based on this idea of the Wisdom Economy you end up with, as Pete calls it, 'a wonderful pool of experience'. There's a lived experience you can't buy, that will add value to your organisation and help the team achieve success. During my career I always wanted to meet recruits who had 'future' potential rather than just met the current job opening. Sometimes the timing wasn't right but we'd stay in touch and when there was something suitable it would be a quicker process to get them recruited. I believe you should always be recruiting, whether or not you have a vacancy right now. Dedicate a few hours every month to stay in touch and network with potential 'future' team members.

We need to expect the unexpected, and the team you have now might not be the same team in five years. Pete has learned that structuring the right team can help manage this changing landscape, as well as unexpected challenges that being a leader will throw at you. If you bring in the right people, encourage them, encourage openness, whether you have the same team in five years or a brand-new team of individuals, you will still reach your goal because you've recruited for more than just their knowledge.

HIRE FOR ATTITUDE NOT APTITUDE. WHEN BUILDING A TEAM, FOCUS CAREFULLY ON WHAT TYPE OF INDIVIDUALS WILL MAKE UP YOUR TEAM OR COMMUNITY AS A WHOLE. WHAT DO THEY BRING TO THE TABLE THAT THEY CAN'T PUT IN A CV?

6. SWEAT THE DETAILS

One day, I was on a call with a client, and I asked them, 'How was your morning?'

And she replied, 'Rubbish. Pointless. It just went too quickly. I didn't get anything done.'

'OK, so what did you actually do?'

'Well, I started off with a team meeting, talking about priorities. Then someone came and told me they were leaving so I spent an hour dealing with that. Then I had to do some mentoring, and various other things. By about one o'clock, I actually physically hadn't done anything I wanted to do.'

I paused, 'Wow, what an amazing morning, you got a lot done.'

It frustrates me when people come to me and complain that so much of their day is spent talking or sorting out problems and dealing with unexpected stuff that happens – but that's what leadership is. The higher up you get, the more you have to give your time to others. And you need to embrace this. You've got to show that you're there for your team, and the details that are important to them are just as important to you.

During the pandemic, Mickela Hall-Ramsay decided to deliver mentoring sessions online at nine o'clock at night because she knew it was the only time the young people she was helping could get online and see everyone else's faces – something they were desperately missing at that time. It was a small detail to some, but probably meant a lot to those involved.

The challenge I'm seeing with clients at the moment is that because everything is scheduled into 30- or 60-minute increments we're losing this spontaneity and one-on-one time with people. You don't want your team to feel like they can't speak to you just because they haven't scheduled a call. Remember, the true test of great leadership is how other people experience you.

THE LITTLE THINGS REALLY DO MATTER, HOWEVER TRIVIAL AND WHATEVER TIME OF THE DAY. WHAT'S IMPORTANT TO OTHERS SHOULD BE IMPORTANT TO YOU. YES, SET BOUNDARIES SO YOU DON'T END UP OVERWORKING YOURSELF, BUT DO WHAT YOU NEED TO DO TO DEMONSTRATE YOU ARE THERE FOR THE PEOPLE YOU LEAD.

7. ASSUME EXCELLENCE NOT INCOMPETENCE

When I first set up my consultancy, I was invited to a presentation by Richard Gerver,[7] a bestselling author and world-renowned thinker. It was there I first heard about 'The Assumption of Excellence' vs. 'The Assumption of Incompetence'. It takes the idea that some leaders tend to assume their teams are incompetent. They think, 'My team doesn't know anything, I have to teach them everything. I've got to keep them motivated and keep them working.' They believe they have to try and be the cleverest person in the room, always challenging and giving opinions.

7 Richard Gerver | Keynote Speaker, Thinker, Educator

He says, switch that around and assume that everyone is excellent. Give your team the tools they need to be excellent, create an environment that fosters excellence, give them clear goals and let them go for it.

Obviously, if you miss a target or something goes wrong you have to manage it, but assuming excellence means you're giving licence to people to be curious and learn. Treat your team like the educated, skilled adults they are. If your team feels they must run everything by you, it tells them you don't trust them.

It's a really expensive mistake to make as a leader if you don't trust your team; the amount of energy, time and money you'll spend on micromanaging people is just crazy. Don't be that person who walks around the office to see who's still there – that's wasting time that could be spent mentoring or building relationships. Don't be that person who asks their staff to record themselves working just to prove they're online – that's wasting time and money on software and will make your staff feel like children. If you bring someone in who has the skills and attitude your organisation needs, but you put constraints on them, they'll start looking for the exit.

An assumption of excellence means you have to be clear you're giving your team a lot of trust; you're empowering them with a lot of responsibility to run their own projects in their own way. But if something goes wrong, and you find out they haven't been doing work they should have been, you're going to want to know and tear everything apart to see what went wrong. It's like running a car: when everything goes well you don't have a reason to look under the bonnet. But as soon as something breaks, you have to take a closer look.

“

YOU ONLY LOOK UNDER THE BONNET when something goes wrong.

IT STARTS WITH YOU. A CULTURE OF TRUST AND EXCELLENCE BEGINS WITH THE GUIDELINES YOU PUT IN PLACE. SO, TREAT PEOPLE LIKE ADULTS. TRUST THEIR ABILITIES AND SKILLS AND GIVE THEM TOOLS TO SUCCEED. IF YOU FIND PEOPLE ARE ASKING YOU FOR PERMISSION, OR ASKING YOU TO CHECK THEIR WORK, SOMETHING HAS GONE WRONG AND YOU NEED TO ADDRESS IT.

8. HOLDING UP THE SHIT UMBRELLA

Managing upwards is an art. If the top of an organisation is dysfunctional then it's tough to have a functional workplace. Just like a family, if there are two fighting parents at the top, the kids will reflect the animosity. Therefore, it's your job as a leader to make sure everything that's coming down and hitting you – whether it's investors, advisers, other board members, your family, whatever it might be – to hold up an umbrella and protect your team from that. If your team is to focus on doing their jobs, it's your job to be the filter and make sure they only hear what they need to. The worst leaders are those who don't have an umbrella and let everything just rain down onto their team. And I'm sure we've all experienced that before. They'll say, 'Oh God, the chairman wants all these stats by the end of the day, and you're gonna have to help me do it. Blame him, not me.' Sound familiar? To me that's poor leadership. Doing this ultimately gives the impression that you're not in control as the leader, because you're just ticking boxes for the people above you. It puts you in a vulnerable position because people will push back when they realise you don't really have much authority. It's a tough job being stuck in the middle as a leader, deciding what should be shared and what shouldn't, but your job is to find the balance and keep your team motivated.

The last few years have been difficult. Lines between work and home are blurred, and people do want leaders to be more honest. There's nothing wrong with this, it builds trust, but draw the line on passing blame from above. If you find you're not happy holding up the shit umbrella, and you know values from above don't align with yours, then it's time to leave. You need to be an authentic leader, too, not just someone's parrot repeating what your bosses tell you.

STEP 1. **REALISE AND ACCEPT THAT HOLDING UP THE SHIT UMBRELLA IS PART OF A LEADER'S JOB.**

STEP 2. **OWN THE INFORMATION YOU COMMUNICATE. SO BE CAREFUL WHAT YOU CHOOSE TO SHARE.**

STEP 3. **DON'T BLAME. ALWAYS SUPPORT THE HIGHER DECISION. IF YOU DON'T BELIEVE IN WHAT YOU IMPLEMENT, DON'T PASS THAT DOWN AND FIND ANOTHER WAY TO COMMUNICATE.**

“

MANAGING UPWARDS IS AN ART. Your role is to hold up an umbrella and protect your team.

AWARENESS

EMPATHY

AWARENESS

1. SELF-APPRAISAL

Self-appraisal is all about self-care and understanding your mental and emotional health. If someone is late to your meeting, why are you annoyed by that? Are you in a good mood today, and why? It's easier to be a supportive and compassionate leader if you're aware of what affects your own mental and emotional state. It's not about sharing your problems, but about opening up and letting people know who you are; what's happening outside of work, your hobbies and interests. So, when you do need to be more vulnerable, when you have those moments of fear or self-doubt, it'll be easier for your team to understand. No one wants to be led by a robot.

During the pandemic Mickela Hall-Ramsay was dealing with a 'neighbour from hell', which meant she was in and out of police stations and courtrooms, and even ended up in hospital due to stress. While she admits she can be a closed book sometimes, she knew this situation called for her to be more transparent with her team – they needed to understand why she might be grumpy one day, why a smile might seem forced, or why she was taking time off. As a result, once they knew the situation, they were empathetic and wanted to help her more, too.

“

PUT ON YOUR OWN OXYGEN MASK BEFORE HELPING THE PERSON NEXT TO YOU. You need to be in a good place before you can help others.

If you have something going on, tell your team so they understand. Say, 'Listen I'm telling you this so you know I've got some personal stuff going on. But I am still here for you. I might take some time off but I am still contactable, and I will help you.'

Let them know who will cover for you and how they can reach you if they need you. It's like the example of putting on your own oxygen mask on a plane before helping the person next to you. You need to be in a good place before you can help others.

GIVE PEOPLE YOU TRUST THE FREEDOM TO TELL YOU WHEN YOU'RE NOT ON YOUR GAME AND ASK THEM FOR FEEDBACK REGULARLY. LET PEOPLE SEE YOUR HUMAN SIDE, SO WHEN YOU NEED TO TAKE A STEP BACK YOUR TEAM WILL HAVE CONTEXT AND INSIGHT TO UNDERSTAND WHY AND BE EMPATHETIC.

2. VULNERABILITY

On Christmas Day, 2019, José Mourinho walked into the changing rooms at Tottenham Football Club to speak to the team. As their manager he was expected to behave a certain way, and his team looked to him for guidance. But that morning something was different. He was in an unusually bad mood. So bad that the people around him knew that something major must have happened. But instead of keeping quiet, he turned to his team, held his hands up and explained that his dog had died.[8]

To some people that might be a trivial thing, and a lot of leaders probably wouldn't even bother explaining themselves. But he chose to say it so his colleagues could understand why he was going to be in that mood. It was such an important moment for the people under his leadership, and it helped his team to know they were not the reason he was upset that day.

It's a fine line between sharing your problems and being a leader who is always telling everyone how stressed they are. But having a leader who is open about their vulnerabilities can foster psychological safety and destigmatise things that sadly often lead to exclusion in the workplace. You can't create a safe and inclusive culture if the boss projects a bulletproof image of themselves. Don't be afraid to be a bit more vulnerable.

But at the same time, don't use it as a tool to manipulate. Vulnerability might be a buzzword at the moment, but don't use it for personal gain. I would always encourage you to be vulnerable, but just be careful with when and how – and what you expect to happen when you are.

8 https://www.thesun.co.uk/sport/football/12576743/spurs-doc-jose-mourinho-dog-died-christmas-eve/ Jose Mourinho cries after his dog dies, Tottenham players react – Spurs Amazon Documentary | Troll Football

REMEMBER THAT EVERYONE IS WATCHING AND LISTENING TO SEE HOW YOU ACT. IF YOU'RE HAVING A TOUGH TIME, THEN SHARE IT. BUT NEVER USE IT AS AN EXCUSE FOR POOR BEHAVIOUR. AND IF THINGS REALLY ARE TOO MUCH, THEN IT'S TIME TO REASSESS WHAT'S IN YOUR CONTROL AND WHETHER YOU ARE BETTER STEPPING BACK OR OUT OF YOUR LEADERSHIP ROLE.

"

IF I CAN SHOW MY VULNERABILITIES TO MY TEAM, IT ENCOURAGES THEM. THEY KNOW THAT THEY ARE SAFE AND SECURE IN THEIRS.
I think irrespective of what sector I worked in, I would always want to foster that.

—Pete Wallroth

3. BURNOUT

I'm not a medical professional, but I've always thought of burnout as having emotional tiredness. When you get absolutely exhausted, when you hate getting up in the morning and you don't want to do anything.

Dr. Eunice Ndirangu-Mugo told me about the time she had to be taken to hospital by one of her friends because she was having dizzy spells. The doctors did every test you can do but they said, 'You don't have any readings that are anywhere near abnormal. You're just tired.' She was ordered to rest and that was the moment the idea of self-care clicked.

'Now,' she says, 'I am very, very intentional about it. I can actually go on leave and not open my laptop. If one of my colleagues calls me for a meeting, I say "No". Every month I take a day out, especially if I feel exhausted. I don't wait to take a vacation anymore. I've learned a lot about the need to take care of myself and to be extremely intentional about it.'

We're seeing more burnout at the moment because leaders' worries have been magnified, thanks both to the changes the pandemic brought as well as the ensuing economic and social challenges. For those leaders who are truly caring and empathetic, it's been especially tough. If you work in traditionally empathetic sectors like medicine, charity, housing or mental health it can be hard to switch off.

Part of the challenge of setting up a company, charity or community is that you can quickly forget why you started. You get overwhelmed by the day-to-day and you lose sight of the original vision – and of yourself.

An exercise I do quite a lot with my clients is to look back at the positives in the last 12 months. It's amazing how much we all focus on what we do wrong. We have a great ability to forget about all the positive things we've achieved, so it's important to look back at some of these and remember why you're leading.

STEP 1. **TAKE CARE OF YOURSELF FIRST. YOU CAN'T LEAD AND LOOK AFTER OTHERS EFFECTIVELY IF YOU'RE BURNT OUT AND STRESSED.**

STEP 2. **MAKE SURE YOU'VE GOT A SAFE PLACE TO GO AND DECOMPRESS. IT'S NOT JUST ABOUT HAVING A GOOD WORK-LIFE BALANCE, IT MEANS SCHEDULE TIME AWAY TO DO SOMETHING THAT'S JUST FOR YOU. ONLY *YOU*. YOU MIGHT FEEL GUILTY BUT DO IT. IT'S CRITICAL.**

STEP 3. **CELEBRATE THE POSITIVES. LOOK BACK AT WHAT YOU'VE LEARNED AND REMEMBER HOW YOU MOVED FORWARD IN THE MIDST OF ADVERSITY. PROBLEMS ARE SIMPLY SPEED BUMPS IN THE ROAD, YOU EVENTUALLY GET OVER THEM. BUT THEY SHOULD NEVER BE A REASON TO STOP OR TURN AROUND!**

STEP 4. **IF YOU'RE TRULY BURNT OUT AND IT'S A REAL PROBLEM (YOU CAN'T SLEEP AT NIGHT AND YOUR RELATIONSHIPS ARE STRUGGLING), THEN IT'S OK TO GET HELP FROM A PROFESSIONAL.**

“

SPEED BUMPS ARE NOT A REASON TO TURN AROUND – eventually you get over them.

4. OFF DAYS

I absolutely stand by the fact that as a leader you're always 'on'. But a prerequisite for being a leader means you will have off days. You have a million things going on, and so many people that you help, it's inevitable. If you have an unplanned off day (you made a mistake, or were rude) make sure you rectify it and apologise. If you're a REAL. leader, and people know what you stand for, they'll understand. If you've got a challenging few weeks coming up and it's going to affect your work – and it's not something you want to share with your whole team – take some time out. Tell one trusted team member and ask them to step in for you.

One of my current clients runs a large tech company. If he wakes up in the morning and knows he's not on his game, he contacts his team and says, 'I'm not coming into the office today, I need to get things sorted and my head straight,' and his team respects that. It doesn't mean he's not contactable, or not working, it just means he's prioritising his needs for that day. He once cancelled a session with me, saying, 'I've decided I just need to do my own stuff today.'

I said, 'Well, talking to me should be helping you with that.'

He agreed, but declined, 'I just know that on these days, I need to take time for myself.'

Obviously not every leader has the luxury of doing that, but you've got to recognise on some days, you won't be perfect – you're only human.

However, that doesn't mean you're allowed to be unpredictable. You can't be in a good mood some days, and in a terrible mood on others. The worst kind of leader is one that people can't trust. So, if you have an off day, or you know you will in the coming weeks, do something about it.

STEP 1. **RECOGNISE WHEN AN OFF DAY IS HAPPENING AND EMBRACE IT. REALISE FOR WHATEVER REASON YOUR HEAD IS NOT IN THE GAME TODAY, AND THAT'S JUST PART OF THE JOB.**

STEP 2. **BE HONEST ABOUT IT. WHETHER YOU PRE-EMPT IT, WHETHER YOU TELL SOMEONE SPECIFICALLY, OR WHETHER YOU ANNOUNCE IT TO LOTS OF PEOPLE, COMMUNICATE IT SO PEOPLE UNDERSTAND.**

STEP 3. **IF YOU UPSET SOMEONE, OR IF YOU MAKE A MISTAKE, APOLOGISE. RECTIFY IT OR FIX IT AS SOON AS YOU CAN.**

5. MAKING MISTAKES

As children we made mistakes all the time. It's how we learned. But as we get older, it gets tougher to make mistakes, especially in business. Failure makes us reluctant to take risks because there are so many people involved who might be affected by our actions. But it's only when you make mistakes, and then rectify them, that it helps your development as a leader. In some ways, your failure can inspire success when everyone can learn from it.

If you make a mistake it really comes down to this: what type of leader have you been? Can your team forgive this mistake? How will you react to this mistake and what will you do to fix it? It's why being an authentic and empathetic leader is so important from day one. We've all seen examples of founders and CEOs being forced out of their companies for unforgivable behaviour.

Don't be *afraid* to make mistakes either, that's just as bad. I've had situations where people in my team were afraid of telling me when something had gone wrong (I talk more about this in 'Avoid an Ostrich Culture'). I realised it was because they were trying to sort out the problem themselves, thinking that admitting it to me would be a sign of weakness. It showed me that I had to change the culture and create a safer environment. If there was a problem it was better to have lots of heads thinking about how to fix it – including mine – rather than letting them stress about it alone.

STEP 1. **BUILD UP YOUR LEADERSHIP PROFILE. PROVE TO PEOPLE THAT YOU ARE AN AUTHENTIC, EMPATHETIC AND TRUSTWORTHY LEADER, SO IF YOU DO HAPPEN TO MAKE A MISTAKE, YOU HAVE SOME LEEWAY.**

STEP 2. **OWN IT. IF YOU MAKE A MISTAKE, HOLD YOUR HANDS UP AND TAKE RESPONSIBILITY.**

STEP 3. **RECTIFY IT. GENUINELY APOLOGISE FOR THE ERROR AND TELL PEOPLE HOW YOU'RE GOING TO FIX IT. DON'T DWELL ON IT.**

"

LEADERS NEED TO LEARN TO FORGIVE THEMSELVES A LITTLE AND CUT THEMSELVES A BIT OF SLACK. You will not be perfect. You will make mistakes. And it's OK if you're learning from them. Take responsibility and seek to do better.

—Dr. Eunice Ndirangu-Mugo

6. AVOID AN OSTRICH CULTURE

Don't bury your head in the sand if things go wrong. I see this happening quite often in successful organisations, as well as those that are more challenged. All leaders, whether they're good or bad, tend to do this. Either because they don't want to let people down, or they just don't want to face the consequences.

One of my coaching clients, Michelle, currently works for a non-government organisation and they're working with a company where all they wanted to hear was good news. I'd been coaching her to speak up more, because she's always left to deal with the fallout of problems later on instead of addressing them in the room.

She was in one of her usual meetings where they would tell the client that everything was fine. Even her bosses were saying everything looked great. But, ultimately, she was responsible for the project's success and she knew that things were not fine. And, as it transpired, she chose that meeting to be honest.

'Actually,' she interrupted, 'I have to say … it's not fine. This is wrong.' She could feel her boss glaring at her and she saw the look on her client's face. But the client actually said, 'Thank you. I now feel like I'm getting the real picture here. I've always wondered whether things were quite as smooth as you were telling me.'

There's always pressure as a leader to take the burden of responsibility alone, and it's a real challenge for organisations to find the balance. It will depend on the culture of your organisation and the work you do. You don't want to be the person who's always talking doom and gloom, but burying your head in the sand doesn't help anyone.

STEP 1. **PUT SYSTEMS IN PLACE TO HELP PEOPLE FEEL SAFE AND COMFORTABLE TO COME TO YOU WHEN THINGS GO WRONG.**

STEP 2. **BE AWARE OF HOW YOU REACT WHEN PEOPLE BRING THESE PROBLEMS OR ISSUES TO YOU. CONTROL YOUR IMPULSE TO CRITICISE OR BLAME PEOPLE; CELEBRATE AND THANK THEM INSTEAD.**

STEP 3. **DON'T HIDE THE PROBLEM BUT TURN IT AROUND AND INVOLVE LOTS OF PEOPLE IN FINDING A SOLUTION.**

AUTHENTICITY

“

LEADERS CAN COME IN ALL SHAPES AND SIZES. But good leadership is always built on authenticity.

—Alex Stephany

AUTHENTICITY

1. WHAT IS AN AUTHENTIC LEADER?

In the past, authenticity didn't seem to matter so much. Most organisations were run by leaders who probably weren't truly themselves. Now, that's changing. People are demanding more dependable leaders and want to join organisations where leaders embody the purpose of their mission. That means as a REAL. leader you've got to be true to who you are and what you believe in.

Think of authentic leadership as connecting your personality with your role. When I go running in the morning, I often run past a pub that has broken glass littered outside it. I always think, 'That'd be a real pain in the arse if, on your commute to work, you get a puncture.' It's six o'clock in the morning and it's not my job but I can't run past it without just pushing the glass to the side. When I told my son about it he asked, 'Why? It's not your job. You didn't put it there and smash it. You're not getting any credit for moving it.'

'I know,' I said, 'I just feel better for doing it.'

That's what being authentic is. I'm not doing it for anybody else. Nobody sees me do it. This is part of who I am. For an authentic leader there is no difference between personal and professional authenticity, and it's not something you can switch on and off.

If you don't believe in what you're doing, if your role feels morally wrong, then it's on you to do something about that. Your actions need to follow your words. Your organisation needs to follow your values. And to me that means doing the right thing even when no one is watching.

Patagonia, an outdoor clothing company, is known as being one of the most authentic businesses, because everything they do ties back to their core values of doing good and running a socially responsible business. During The Black Friday sales in 2021, they announced they'd give away any profit they made, over their usual amount, to charity. It was during the Covid-19 pandemic, and times were tough for everybody, but during the sale they ended up getting ten times their normal revenue on that one day. The first thing they did was to keep their word and give it all away. *All ten times their revenue went to charity as promised.* There was no question that they weren't going to do that. You can imagine other companies might have squirmed and tried to go back on their promise. And now Patagonia's founder, Yvon Chouinard, has pledged to give away his fortune to help efforts to save the planet.[9]

There are going to be situations, of course, where you will have to compromise. You have salaries to pay or decisions that are out of your control. Authentic leadership means moderating your personal beliefs and behaviours for the needs of your team, for the organisation you're leading and for the mission you're all working towards, together. This isn't your opportunity to say, 'Right, I'm the leader, this is how it's

9 Yvon Chouinard Donates Patagonia to Fight Climate Crisis

going to be,' because that borders on narcissism or a dictatorship. Authenticity doesn't give you carte blanche to do or say whatever you want. It's not an excuse for poor leadership.

You are never going to be perfectly authentic, but it's how you react when compromises happen that determines how authentic a leader you are going to be. And sometimes it means you'll be unpopular, too. If you're truly being authentic to yourself, you're not going to please everybody and that's part of the job.

LEADERS SHOULD ALWAYS BE TRUE TO WHO THEY ARE AND TO THEIR VALUES. BRINGING A TRUE VERSION OF YOURSELF TO WORK IS WHAT AUTHENTIC LEADERSHIP IS ABOUT. YOU CAN'T SWITCH IT ON OR OFF AND IT STARTS FROM DAY ONE. IF YOU DON'T FEEL YOU CAN BE TRUE TO YOURSELF THEN PERHAPS IT'S TIME TO QUESTION WHETHER YOU SHOULD BE IN THAT ROLE OR IN THAT ORGANISATION.

2. YOUR VALUES

In 2018, the actress Roseanne Barr put out a racist tweet[10] about one of Barack Obama's senior aides. Robert Iger was the chair of Disney at the time, which was the parent company of ABC, which produced her work.

The backlash on Twitter was huge, and ABC was under pressure to respond. According to Iger's book, *The Ride of a*

10 https://www.nytimes.com/2018/05/29/business/media/roseanne-barr-offensive-tweets.html

Lifetime, he was under pressure from the board *not* to fire her. She'd been there longer than he had and she was an 'institution'. But in a statement he said, 'There was only one thing to do here, and that was the right thing.' She was fired, and her sitcom on ABC was cancelled. Even though it had the highest ratings of any new TV show in years and brought in millions of dollars in advertising, he had to make a decision that was in line with the values of his organisation.

Sticking to your values as a leader is not a case of just writing values up on the wall or sticking it on your website; you've got to live and breathe it every day. On the good days and the bad. And when you're a leader, there's very little difference between your personal values and your business values; being authentic means sticking to them, just as Robert Iger did.

When people work for a truly authentic leader, with clear values, they'll often give their whole hearts and minds to the cause. Teamwork and loyalty spreads, resulting in high morale and producing extraordinary results. So does your team know what your values are? Can you see them living them through their behaviours and communication?

If you can't be true to your values, then it's time to be honest with yourself about how and why that is – and what needs to change.

STEP 1. DEFINE YOUR VALUES. CRYSTALLISE THEM. MAKE SURE YOUR BRANDING, MARKETING, CUSTOMER SERVICE, *EVERYTHING*, COMMUNICATES IT JUST AS CLEARLY.

STEP 2. MAKE VALUES ACTIONABLE. IF YOU WANT YOUR TEAM TO FOLLOW YOU AND HELP YOU MAKE AN IMPACT, THEN YOU'VE GOT TO HELP THEM FIND WAYS TO IMPLEMENT THOSE VALUES THROUGH THEIR BEHAVIOUR AND ACTIONS.

STEP 3. IF YOU EVER FAIL IN LIVING UP TO YOUR VALUES – YOUR BEHAVIOUR DOESN'T MATCH THEM OR YOU SAID SOMETHING WRONG – IT'S HOW YOU FIRST RESPOND TO THAT MISTAKE THAT MATTERS.

3. THE STORYTELLER-IN-CHIEF

An inspiring leader is someone who can create a story, a creative vision that compels you to follow them. When people are anxious and living in uncertain times – as we are now – people want leaders who can tell stories of a better future. People want to feel comforted by their leaders, and know they are in good hands. You don't always have to have the answer, sometimes it's just reassuring people that you're working on finding it. You're looking for a better solution.

Alex Stephany is a great example of a leader with a story:

> 'I became friends with a homeless man who sat outside my local tube station in London. I'd buy him cups of coffee and pairs of socks when it was getting cold. At one point, he disappeared for weeks on end. When he reappeared, he looked years older: he told me he'd had a heart attack and had just come out of hospital. Despite the well-meaning gestures from myself and no doubt others, he was in a worse position than ever.

> So I began to ask myself what it would take to make a lasting difference to this man's life. He had never had a job and was illiterate. For me, the answer lay in empowering him with the skills and training needed to sustainably support himself. Of course, that would cost far more than coffees or socks – but what if everyone chipped in?'

And that's how Alex Stephany became the founder and CEO of Beam, an online platform that crowdfunds employment training for homeless people. You can see this story threaded through his marketing. It's what attracts people to his work, and it's what helps to grow his organisation.

But this doesn't mean you now have to have the charisma or communication skills to stand up and tell a story. You don't have to have an epic journey to share or a life-changing moment. When you look at why people join organisations, there's often a spotlight on the senior leadership, the founders and the owners. People want to know who, how and why – that's the story they want.

As the leader you may be a storyteller, but remember the people you lead and inspire are also intertwined with your story. They are the supporting characters, the bit-part players and the extras. You are all telling the story together.

STEP 1. **UNDERSTAND THAT PEOPLE WANT HUMAN LEADERS. THEY WANT TO UNDERSTAND WHY YOU LEAD LIKE YOU DO, WHAT YOUR STORY IS AND WHY YOU CARE. AND THAT MEANS BEING MORE OPEN AND APPROACHABLE IN YOUR LEADERSHIP.**

STEP 2. **IT'S NOT ABOUT BEING THE MOST CHARISMATIC, RUNNING THE BEST COMPANY OR BEING THE MOST CONFIDENT. IT'S ABOUT JUST SPEAKING SINCERELY AND AUTHENTICALLY ABOUT YOUR WORK.**

STEP 3. **IF PEOPLE ARE ANXIOUS AND UNCERTAIN. BE THE COMFORT AND STABILITY THEY ARE LOOKING FOR.**

“

THE MORE YOU CAN BE AUTHENTIC, THE HAPPIER YOU’RE GOING TO BE, and life will work itself around that.

—Melinda French Gates, American philanthropist, former multimedia product developer and manager at Microsoft

CONNECTING

AUTHENTICITY

CONNECTING

1. LEADING IS TALKING

One of my clients, Victoria, was always that kind of person who was great at getting stuff done. She was the one who would do the final report and was known for running projects and bringing it all together. But for her to step up and become an effective leader, she realised she had to be more of a people person. Rather than being super-efficient and organised, she needed to take the time to understand her team, their motivations and how to inspire them. She had to learn how to factor in time to socialise and chit-chat.

One of the most important things you must do as a leader is to show your authenticity and, in some cases, personal vulnerability. And that means making time just to talk, just to share, because we're all in this together. You must build genuine connections with your staff. You can't fake interest in them. Good leadership isn't just about writing reports or putting out fires. It's about being there for your people. Making small talk is what builds a bridge with your team.

When I worked with Victoria, we looked at her workload and saw where she could fit in more time to do it, and I suggest you do the same. When you book in your meetings, always book in an extra half hour or so to catch up and talk to people.

You need to make time for those impromptu conversations. You might think you haven't got anything done in terms of actual tasks, but if you've spent the day talking to people, helping them and motivating them, then that's being a leader.

STEP 1. **MAKE SOCIALISING AND CONNECTING A DAILY HABIT. EVEN IN EMAILS, ON CALLS AND IN MEETINGS. IT'S NOT ABOUT TALKING TO EVERYONE BECAUSE YOU HAVE TO TICK A BOX, IT'S ABOUT CREATING A CULTURE AROUND AUTHENTICALLY CONNECTING WITH EACH OTHER.**

STEP 2. **IF YOU'RE UNCOMFORTABLE, PREPARE QUESTIONS AND PRACTISE IN ADVANCE. ASK OPEN-ENDED QUESTIONS THAT ALLOW OTHER PEOPLE TO TELL YOU MORE ABOUT THEMSELVES.**

STEP 3. **REMEMBER TO FIND AND TALK TO THE PEOPLE WHO NEED IT MOST. THEY MIGHT NOT ALWAYS BE THE ONES YOU EXPECT.**

2. HOW TO CREATE A SAFE SPACE

A safe space is an environment where people can talk to you without fear. Somewhere they can express their emotions, their opinions, and even criticise, without any kind of judgement or retribution. You create one through your communication and actions, your focus on the person in front of you, your ability to listen and care, by controlling your impulses. Someone once said to me that when they came and talked to me, it felt like being wrapped in a blanket; they didn't have to worry about saying the wrong thing. And I think that's what a safe space is. People should be able to come to you and honestly say, 'You've got that wrong,' or 'I'm upset with what that person is saying.' It's hugely important, especially in the current environment where there's so much uncertainty about what's right or wrong, what's acceptable and what's not.

The challenge for you is the success of a safe space depends so much on how you react and how you feel. It's only as safe as you make it. If you react in a bad way, if you judge and you think, 'Right, I'm going to get you for saying that,' it's going to fail. It's tough. Creating a safe space is a lot about getting yourself in the right frame of mind to hold a safe space for others; I've had times where people have said things to me and I've just been distraught afterwards. You've got to be psychologically ready to take it. This is why I talk so much about self-awareness earlier in the book.

A useful method I use is to ask the person coming to me, 'What's the outcome you want from me today?' Many people want to express their opinions openly, so you have to manage the conversation to get the result your team needs. Ask them, 'Is this going to be a discussion where you simply want to vent and express your frustration? Or do you want me to do something?' When I know that, I can consciously prepare.

If someone's just coming to vent then I switch into 'listening mode': *I'm listening. I'm empathising, I'm hearing you.* If they want me to act and do something about it, I'm going to be processing: *Right, this is what I'm going to do next. This is what I have to action.*

STEP 1. **BE WILLING TO TALK, TO LISTEN AND TO TAKE ACTION IF NEEDED. THERE'S NO POINT IN HAVING A SAFE SPACE IF NOTHING COMES FROM IT.**

STEP 2. **IT'S GOING TO BE UNCOMFORTABLE. IT'S GOING TO BE TOUGH. EMBRACE IT. THINK ABOUT HOW YOU'RE GOING TO ACT AND WHAT YOU'RE GOING TO SAY. BE READY TO HEAR SOME TOUGH FEEDBACK AND DON'T TAKE IT PERSONALLY.**

STEP 3. **INVEST IN YOUR SENIOR TEAM AND MAKE SURE THEY CAN CREATE THESE SAFE SPACES, TOO.**

“

WHEN YOU CAN DISAGREE WITH YOUR COLLEAGUES AND EVEN YOUR LEADER WITHOUT ANY FEAR OF VICTIMISATION, it’s a sign of a psychologically safe place to work.

—Allaya Cooks-Campbell,
L&D Specialist at BetterUp,
SEO Storyteller for Wellness Brands

“

TO TAME YOUR MAMMOTH, STOP BEING THE PERSON OTHER PEOPLE THINK YOU SHOULD BE, and be the person you want to be.

3. TAMING THE MAMMOTH

Taming The Mammoth – from a blog by Tim Urban[11] – is such a great idea. 'The Mammoth' is the irrational and unproductive obsession we all have with what you believe people are thinking and saying about you. And it's something we all carry around. When you get imposter syndrome in a meeting, it's your mammoth behind you saying, 'You can't do this. They're laughing at you, you don't know what you're doing.'

One of my clients, Joanne, made a mistake on a project early on in her career. It wasn't a catastrophic mistake, but it did mean the client got really angry and her boss had to step in. Ever since then – and we're talking over ten years ago – she overcompensates massively. Every time her boss asks to speak to her, she thinks she's going to get fired. Every time she makes a mistake she gets upset because she thinks she'll get fired. Consequently, she doesn't ask for help, gets overwhelmed and by then it's too late. She carries her mammoth around with her every day even though it doesn't help her. Her fear of failure was becoming debilitating and it's something we had to work hard on.

To tame your mammoth, stop being the person other people think you should be; be the person you want to be. Be honest about who you are and what's important to you – be your authentic self. As leaders we can spend too long worrying about what people will think, what you should say or how you should act. Your mammoth craves approval, but that's not how you become a REAL. Leader. Effective

11 Why You Should Stop Caring What Other People Think (Taming the Mammoth) – Wait But Why https://waitbutwhy.com/2014/06/taming-mammoth-let-peoples-opinions-run-life.html

leadership isn't a popularity contest. It's a tough job and sometimes that means doing things that scare you.

STEP 1. **REMEMBER, YOUR FEARS ARE IRRATIONAL. YOU MAY THINK PEOPLE ARE TALKING ABOUT YOU, BUT IN REALITY MOST PEOPLE ARE TOO BUSY THINKING ABOUT THEMSELVES, OR ABOUT WHAT YOU THINK OF THEM.**

STEP 2. **IT'S COUNTERPRODUCTIVE TO TRY AND FIT IN. WHEN YOU ARE YOUR AUTHENTIC SELF, YOU WILL HAVE MORE ORIGINAL THOUGHTS AND IDEAS. YOU ARE ALSO MORE LIKELY TO MAKE AN IMPACT AND CREATE CHANGE WHEN YOU CAN BE YOURSELF.**

STEP 3. **BE COURAGEOUS. NOTHING YOU'RE SOCIALLY SCARED OF IS ACTUALLY GOING TO HURT YOU. STAND UP AND MAKE BOLD CHOICES, AND YOU'LL WEAKEN THAT MAMMOTH.**

4. THE GOOD, THE BAD AND THE UGLY

During the pandemic, one of my clients and his board made the decision to take a significant pay cut. When things are going wrong, it's your job as the leader to stand up and support your team, and in this instance, it was to take action and mitigate the impact of lost revenue on his employee's pay packets. People can tell when leaders are dealing with something that's gone wrong, we've all been in that situation where there are hushed whispers and confused looks. No one wants to follow a pessimist who is constantly telling everyone when things fail, but equally you shouldn't say something is good when it's clearly not. Have faith in yourself and your team's abilities to pull together and improve a bad situation. Be optimistic when challenges arise; it's what leadership is all about. But don't be dishonest. If things are getting difficult, share it with your team. They'll find out anyway, so it'll sound better coming directly from you. I'm not saying you should take a pay cut every time costs get high, but find actionable ways to keep team morale up. This is where having a good board of directors or a senior team can help you. Have people around you, mentors or coaches who you can go to and say, 'Listen, this is our challenge. What can I do?' I remember a time when my company decided we needed to cut costs. It was mandated from above and it seemed inevitable that we would have to cut our headcount. I initially spent a few sleepless nights trying to find a solution, but I eventually shared the challenge with my senior team. They came back to me with some brilliant (but tough) solutions, and we avoided losing people.

STEP 1. **YOUR JOB IS TO BE OPTIMISTIC, BUT NOT DISHONEST. KEEP PEOPLE INFORMED.**

STEP 2. **BE HUMBLE. UNDERSTAND THAT PEOPLE MIGHT BE ABLE TO HELP YOU IF YOU CONFIDE IN THEM.**

STEP 3. BE AWARE OF NON-VERBAL COMMUNICATION. WHAT YOU *DON'T* SAY, AND HOW YOU ACT HOLDS AS MUCH WEIGHT AS YOUR WORDS.

5. BE SINCERE OR DON'T BOTHER

In June 2022, the head of a regional water company was featured on the national news for failing to provide water to their local area. I expected him to appear and read a note his marketing team had given him. I expected him to be insincere. But actually he surprised me. He took the video call in his house and said, 'Look, I'm really sorry, all I know is we're trying our best, and we're doing our best to get you back up. But we're going to keep the free water going and hand out water bottles for a few more days.'

You could tell it wasn't scripted as it came across as honest and sincere, and that's so important. Sincerity is a core part of authenticity, you can't have one without the other. We've all seen bosses of companies where they've had somebody – maybe in marketing or PR – write a script for them. And then they stand up and read all the words someone else has written; there's nothing *less* motivating. People are looking for sincerity and authenticity in every single word. There's nothing wrong with reading a script, but you've got to make it authentic in your own way, otherwise it won't have the desired impact. And if you can't put something into your own words, if you can't put your feelings into it, then don't do it. Let someone else say it for you.

As I said at the start of this book, the power has shifted. The world has become more transparent. We expect leaders to be more accountable than before and people will have no fear about calling you out. If you say your organisation will do something, and then it doesn't do it, everyone will talk about it. The number of platforms people can use to communicate is far greater today – and they are a lot more effective. You've got to live and breathe by what you say.

STEP 1. **WHEN YOU COMMUNICATE, SAY WHAT YOU GENUINELY MEAN. DON'T JUST SAY IT FOR THE SAKE OF IT, OR BECAUSE IT'S WHAT YOU'VE BEEN TOLD TO SAY.**

STEP 2. **BE SINCERE WITH YOUR ACTIONS. IF YOU'RE TALKING TO SOMEONE, WAIT FOR THE RESPONSE. LOOK THEM IN THE EYE AND PHYSICALLY BE PRESENT.**

STEP 3. **IF YOU CANNOT BE SINCERE IN THE MOMENT, DON'T SAY ANYTHING AT ALL. BE HONEST AND SAY YOU DON'T KNOW WHAT TO SAY OR TELL PEOPLE YOU'LL COME BACK TO THEM.**

"

AUTHENTICITY IS WHEN you say and do the things you actually believe.

—Simon Sinek

6. CULTURAL AWARENESS

In May of 2021, Jason Fried, the CEO of software company Basecamp, had to apologise after the introduction of a new policy prohibiting 'societal and political discussions' caused a third of his workforce to leave.[12] While it came from a good place in terms of what the company was trying to do, using such a blanket response for every employee didn't work and it caused a huge uproar. Unfortunately, the senior team's response to the uproar was that people were free to leave if they wanted – so a third of the workforce quit.

You can do all the right things in an effort to be authentic, but do one thing wrong and there could be massive consequences for you. Nowadays, everyone's got an opinion about you – and thanks to social media everyone will talk about you. The implications of everything you do will be much, much greater than they ever were before. Therefore, you need to be tolerant of and broad-minded about other views. Your role as leader is to make the culture as open as possible, it's about creating that safe working environment for everyone;

12 An Update (hey.com)

you can't tread on eggshells, constantly worrying about what you're going to say. And make sure you have a team around you to assist with your open culture.

I have a number of clients who have come to me worried about saying the wrong thing. This could be about anything from diversity and inclusion, to how to deal with different generations. Don't assume that setting up a committee is going to fix these issues for you. It's all very well saying you're going to look into your quotas and processes, but it's pointless if it's not going to come from the top; it needs to become part of your ongoing culture. Remember, you may create the culture, but it's also up to both the teams and their managers to maintain it as the organisation grows.

STEP 1. **KEEP LEARNING AND SPEAKING TO PEOPLE AROUND YOU. FIND OUT IF YOU HAVE UNCONSCIOUS BIAS AND CHANGE IT. BE WILLING TO GET CALLED OUT REGULARLY.**

STEP 2. **DON'T REACT TOO QUICKLY. IT'S EASY TO TAKE THINGS PERSONALLY OR JUMP ON THE NEXT TREND BECAUSE IT FEELS OR SOUNDS RIGHT, BUT YOU COULD BE UPSETTING 100 OTHER PEOPLE BY DOING IT. TAKE YOUR TIME AND DON'T RUSH YOUR DECISIONS.**

STEP 3. **DON'T SEE THIS AS ONE POINT IN TIME. PEOPLE CHANGE. BELIEFS CHANGE. OPINIONS CHANGE. THIS IS A JOURNEY AND YOU'LL NEED TO KEEP CHECKING IN REGULARLY.**

7. AVOID FAVOURITISM

Treat everyone with the respect they deserve. That doesn't mean you can't reward those people who work hardest or are most successful, just make sure you are consistent with everyone. Equally, you must act when people are not performing or contributing to be fair on the rest of the team.

Amit used to work in an open-plan office. There were some people he genuinely enjoyed talking to, and others he knew would just vent at him and bring him down. It's difficult because in the morning who are you most likely to want to speak to? But I had to remind him, as a leader, you have to think about your role; you can't single out particular people to spend time with.

Another client, Sarah, brought her husband in to work for her company. While he's very good at his job, and more than qualified, it's causing problems and she's now regretting it. In some situations, it's perfectly reasonable to ask friends and family to help out, especially at the beginning or when you lack resources. But at some point you have to take a step back and think about what's best for the organisation and the people you work with.

You may have certain people that you choose to spend more time with at work, closer friends or colleagues you connect better with. But the days of that have gone. You can't have favourites, you've got to think about how your actions could compromise you being objective and fair – and how people view your leadership. To be successful, you need a team that's motivated and supporting you, and that means treating everybody equally.

MAKE SURE YOU'RE AWARE OF WHAT KIND OF PICTURE YOU'RE PAINTING WITH YOUR LEADERSHIP. BEING A LEADER MEANS YOU'RE DELIBERATELY DIVIDED AND SEPARATE FROM YOUR TEAM. THERE IS A LINE YOU CANNOT CROSS, AND IF YOU FIND YOURSELF OVERSTEPPING IT, OR IF PEOPLE VOICE THEIR CONCERNS OR CALL YOU OUT, THEN YOU HAVE TO ACT ON IT – HOWEVER PAINFUL THAT MIGHT BE.

“

WE TREAT OUR PEOPLE LIKE ROYALTY. If you honour and serve the people who work for you, they will honour and serve you.

—Mary Kay Ash, founder of Mary Kay Cosmetics

“

DON’T RIDE AN EMOTIONAL ROLLERCOASTER

the best leaders always provide stability and safety.

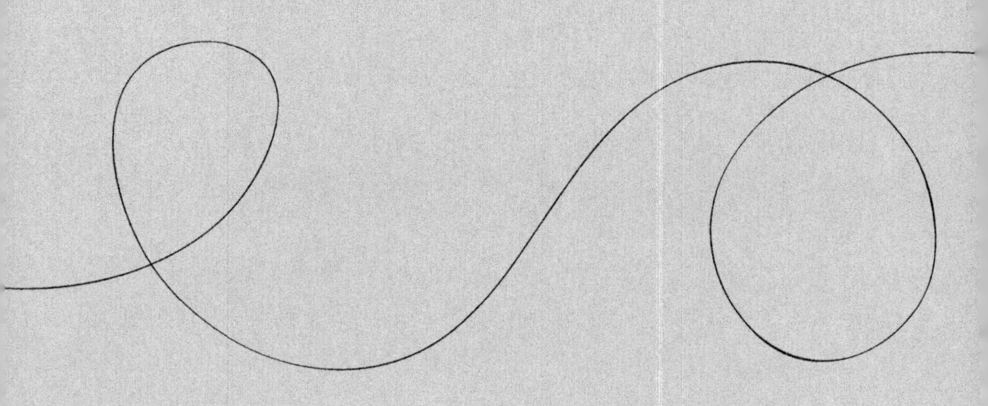

8. DON'T RIDE THE EMOTIONAL ROLLERCOASTER

One of my worst ever bosses was one who led everyone on an emotional rollercoaster. You never knew until she flung open her office door, what mood she was going to be in that day. And it was horrible. That's the worst type of leader to be. It's OK not to be OK sometimes, we all have bad days and feel rubbish. But at work, as in life, we all need stability and safety, and as a leader you have to offer that always – even if you don't feel like it. The best leaders are emotionally consistent and approachable so the team knows where they are with them at all times. You must keep your head when things are going wrong and not send your fears out into the organisation, it can be cancerous. Yes, people want vulnerability from their leaders, but that doesn't mean creating an environment of uncertainty or fear. Choose your moments to be vulnerable – your team still needs to see you as a stable leadership figure. And it's not just you that needs to maintain emotional consistency, your senior team needs to avoid emotional rollercoasters, too. If one of them completely loses their temper with someone, stunning everyone into silence, it's up to you to pull them into a private room immediately to find out what caused the outburst.

It's easy to feel the weight of the world on your shoulders as a leader, you spend all day sorting out everyone else's problems but what about yours? I would always recommend that you have a 'go to' person in your life who you can vent to and share your frustrations with. And I would always make sure to have another outlet, like exercise, socialising with family or friends, or another hobby that allows you to totally switch off.

STEP 1. BE HELD ACCOUNTABLE BY SOMEONE YOU TRUST, WHO WILL TELL YOU WHAT YOU DID WRONG, WHEN YOU GOT EMOTIONAL OR SAID THE WRONG THING.

STEP 2. ALWAYS SHOW PASSION BUT CHANNEL EMOTION INTO THE RIGHT THINGS. IT'S A FINE LINE BETWEEN SHARING YOUR PROBLEMS AND CONCERNS, BUT ALSO NOT MAKING IT TOO EMOTIONAL AND CREATING AN UNSTABLE ENVIRONMENT.

STEP 3. FREQUENT AND CLEAR COMMUNICATION WILL HELP YOUR TEAM UNDERSTAND WHEN THINGS ARE GETTING CHALLENGING. TREAT YOUR COLLEAGUES WITH RESPECT, BE HONEST AND TRANSPARENT AT ALL TIMES.

LONELINESS

AUTHENTICITY

LONELINESS

1. A LONELY PLACE

'There's stuff you just can't share with everybody,' Eunice Ndirangu-Mugo admits. 'So they start wondering; what are you doing?' As a leader the buck stops with you. You're the one that has to make the final decision, to make things happen and sometimes not everyone will be behind you; they will be questioning your decisions. But there's a line you can't cross with your team, a distance you have to maintain if you want to be an effective leader. That means you'll often end up feeling lonely.

But leadership is not a popularity contest. There are going to be times when you will feel like you're constantly making decisions on your own, especially now people are often working remotely, and that social aspect of work isn't quite the same. I used to find that I liked the buzz of people around me. It helped me work and got me through the tough days.

But, 'You've got to block out some of those [negative] voices in your head,' Marc Convey says. In his experience, 'You've got to get through certain periods, show resilience, adaptability and sometimes nip other people's thoughts in their buds. You can't always take on the whole world, or your whole team's problems. And I think that's one of the hardest things about leadership; it can be quite lonely in those spaces.'

This doesn't mean you can't have a good relationship with your team, show vulnerability or admit mistakes; it just means knowing that the final decision is yours, the responsibility ends with you – and that can be a lonely place.

STEP 1. **ACCEPT IT AND EMBRACE IT. THIS IS PART OF THE JOB.**

STEP 2. **BUILD A NETWORK AROUND YOU, OR MAKE SURE YOU HAVE PEOPLE AROUND YOU THAT YOU CAN TALK TO.**

STEP 3. **CONSTANTLY LEARN, READ AND CONSUME. LEARNING FROM OTHERS WILL HELP YOU STAY CONNECTED AND YOU'LL REALISE YOU AREN'T QUITE AS ALONE IN YOUR CHALLENGES AS YOU THINK.**

2. HAVE A SOUNDING BOARD

Where do you go when you're stressed? Who can you talk to when you have anxieties about your time, your work-life balance, or yourself?

Who can you talk to who will give you an honest, independent and most importantly, an *objective* response? Your family will tell you what you want to hear because they love you and want you to do well. But that's not going to help you be a better leader. Investors have money in the business, so can only advise you from their point of view. And the board are all going to be playing politics and everything else that comes with that. You need to have someone truly independent. Who doesn't have any vested interest in the success of your business.

I think anybody in a senior position has got to make sure they have people to go to, and there are two types:

1. Someone within your organisation who can advise you within the constraints of the business and your role. A person who doesn't have a stake in any decisions you make.
2. Someone who is completely independent from you and the organisation, who you trust to be very honest with you, and you with them.

Having a sounding board is probably the most important thing you'll need as a leader. One of my clients came to me because she was 'struggling to see the wood for the trees'. She had to manage multiple stakeholders and a demanding schedule, and was under a lot of pressure. As I had no stake in the business this meant I could see the limiting beliefs and habits she had, and I could reframe situations in ways that helped her find better solutions. When I coach leaders, I give them honest and objective advice because I care about *them* being successful – I don't have any interest in their business. I care about *them* and *their version* of success – whatever it means to them.

If you can't find a sounding board or have no funds to hire a coach, mentors are also great. When you choose a mentor, you're choosing someone who's experienced in a particular thing that you need help with. So, if communication is a massive weakness of yours then find someone who's been a great communicator in your life and ask them if they might mentor you. Remember though, mentoring is a big commitment. It is as much a responsibility of the mentee, as it is the mentor.

DON'T GO TOO CLOSE TO HOME WHEN LOOKING FOR YOUR SOUNDING BOARD. FIND SOMEONE WHO WILL GIVE YOU THAT SAFE SPACE TO TALK THINGS OUT AND ASK THOSE UNCOMFORTABLE QUESTIONS. YOU NEED TO FEEL CONFIDENT THAT THEY'RE NOT GOING TO JUDGE YOU, AND THAT YOU CAN SAY SOMETHING THAT MIGHT BE DIFFICULT TO VERBALISE. THEY NEED TO BE SOMEONE WHO WILL PUSH YOU, CHALLENGE YOU AND HELP YOU 'SEE THE WOOD FOR THE TREES'. IT DOESN'T HAVE TO BE JUST ONE PERSON, EITHER. YOU CAN GET ADVICE FROM LOTS OF DIFFERENT PEOPLE WITH VARYING SKILLS AND EXPERIENCE. YOU'LL DISCOVER THAT LEADERSHIP CHALLENGES ARE ALL INCREDIBLY SIMILAR, AND SPEAKING TO PEOPLE OUTSIDE YOUR SECTOR WILL PROBABLY HELP YOU REALISE YOU AREN'T AS ALONE IN THIS ROLE AS YOU THINK.

3. YES PEOPLE

REAL. leadership is not a popularity contest. Nor is it about being the most beloved person in an organisation. Your role is to make the business successful. That's why you're the leader, and you're never going to grow as a leader if you're never challenged.

I reckon that for pretty much every leader, every board, every senior team, there are lots of 'Yes' people. This goes right back to favouritism, nepotism, cronyism, whatever you want to call it. 'Yes' people do whatever they can to climb up the ladder. And this can be challenging because, as a leader, you want people who say 'Yes', to follow you and agree with your ideas. In fact, lots of leaders are known for being people pleasers; they want to make their teams happy. It's also flattering to have people agree with everything you say.

But having a room full of people saying the same thing, or agreeing with you, is not healthy or helpful for anyone. And it's often the result of a culture set by the leader. If you give the impression you cannot be questioned or that you'll shoot down and ignore any suggestions, then people will fear speaking out. Ultimately, the only way to prevent 'Yes' people is by creating 'psychological safety' to give people the confidence to voice their opinion. A good place to start is to remove dominance from conversations or meetings by offering your own opinion last after encouraging others to contribute.

I once had to restructure a team of 100 people in just two months, and it was not a popular decision. So, I made sure I started with clear over-communication around the goals, and constant updates on how things were going. There was always direct action to keep things moving and an open door at all times for any questions or concerns. (To help myself, I used the Tuckman model I mentioned on page 41.)

STEP 1. SURROUND YOURSELF WITH PEOPLE WHO AREN'T AFRAID TO CHALLENGE YOU.

STEP 2. CREATE A SAFE ENVIRONMENT WHERE PEOPLE CAN DISAGREE WITH YOU WITHOUT REPERCUSSIONS.

STEP 3. BE AWARE OF PEOPLE WHO MAY NOT SPEAK UP AS MUCH. THEY PERHAPS HAVE A DIFFERENT COMMUNICATION STYLE OR FIND IT DIFFICULT TO MAKE THEIR POINT.

4. YOU DON'T HAVE TO BE A SUPERHERO

Indra Nooyi used to be the CEO of PepsiCo. She once recalled a great moment where she was relaxing, working away, while her kids were doing their homework. She was working and getting things done – running Pepsi – but she still got to have her family with her. She called it a 'best' moment and I think it's quite a powerful image; she's not pretending she's one or the other, she's authentically doing both and saying to her family, 'I'm loving being with you. But I'm also happy when I'm doing the work at the same time.' It didn't matter how senior she was, she made her family a priority.

And this is important because it meant everybody else could do that as well. She was inspirational in terms of her authenticity; she didn't hide anything and she didn't try to pretend she was some kind of superwoman. I think now, more than ever, people are trying to figure out the best balance for them. Leaders are being told you 'should' switch off for the holidays, or never work weekends. But if, like Indra Nooyi, the balance isn't one or the other, it's both melded together, then that's OK, too. I have a client who's so obsessed with data that he loves spending his Sunday mornings going through it. And he wouldn't change that for the world. It's how he loves to spend his time.

I'm not saying you have to make a point about having the kids in the office, or shout about how you love working weekends, but it's about doing what feels right for your leadership style.

FIND THAT PLACE WHERE YOU ARE DOING WHAT YOU'RE HAPPY DOING, WITHOUT FEELING APOLOGETIC ABOUT IT. HAVE FAITH IN YOUR ABILITIES AND YOUR CHOICES, WHATEVER THEY MIGHT BE. IT'S REALLY EASY AT THE MOMENT TO GET SWAYED OR QUESTION YOURSELF. YOU DON'T HAVE TO HAVE ALL THE ANSWERS, BUT YOU DO HAVE TO HAVE FAITH IN YOUR DECISIONS.

5. YOU'RE NOT THE ONLY ONE

The number one question I get asked by my clients is, 'What are other leaders going through? Am I the only one?' So, the first thing I would say to you is, 'No, you're not the only one.' When I coach people, I tell stories and share experiences and examples (obviously confidentially!) that I've been through or worked on with various clients. There are some very common themes that have been around for years that don't go away

– imposter syndrome, self-belief, change management, the difference between leading and managing – so be assured that all those kinds of problems are ones all leaders regularly experience.

Carlos Posada (one of our everyday leaders) set up a business in Colombia that buys local farmers' produce and sells it to businesses at a fairer price. One of their biggest problems is that they took on a founder who no longer serves the business effectively – how do they change that? Here in the UK, I am working with a charity and a tech business, two very different organisations, and they also have the same problem as Carlos. It doesn't matter where you are, what size business you have, what you're doing, you'll find that every leader has very similar challenges.

When Pete Wallroth networks with other people in his industry, he's still surprised to learn how similar everyone's experiences are. 'From a leadership perspective it's really interesting,' he says. 'We're all involved in very different organisations and our scales are very different. But I can remember what [a particular] challenge feels like, I can remember the way that I worked it out.' And that's something he can share with someone who is going through it now.

DRAW COMFORT FROM EXTERNAL PEERS OR LEADERS IN OTHER COMPANIES AND INDUSTRIES. THEY WILL ALL BE HAVING THE SAME CHALLENGES AS YOU. IT DOESN'T MATTER WHETHER THEY'RE LEADING ONE PERSON OR ONE THOUSAND, THEY'LL STILL HAVE THE SAME FEARS AND INSECURITIES.

“

Have you reached
A CROSSROADS?

6. FACING THE CROSSROADS

I've got some clients who are at a crossroads, thinking, 'Shit, I need to get out of this. I don't want to push any harder. I don't want to earn any more money, I just want to step out and do something else.' But they don't know what to do.

If you created your business you had a reason to jump out of bed in the morning; it was your baby. But, as time goes by, you may start to realise, 'Wow, I need to scale it, I need to add people, I need to involve other people in this.' And that's usually the time when you start to think, 'Well, am I the right person to be leading this?' You might have a particular skill: you're a technical whizz, you're great at marketing, or sales, or whatever it might be that got your business to this place, but only you can do that assessment and think, 'Am I the right person to actually be leading this team?'

When David came to me he wasn't sure if he wanted to lead because he wasn't enjoying the people management side of it. He was a do-er. He loved doing creative stuff, but now he was running an agency and other people were doing the things he loved. So, the very first thing we needed to pick apart was: did he want to be one of the creatives? Or did he want to lead the business? Because he couldn't do both.

It's that kind of assessment I challenge a lot of my clients to think about, because it's not to say that you can't become a better leader, you absolutely can. But it's whether you really want to. Maybe being the leader is not where you're best used within your business. After helping David, he still says to me now he's not sure what type of leader he is (or wants to be). I don't think he's truly found out yet, but that's OK. He's changed the way he manages people, and he's in a much more comfortable space. It's an admirable quality when, as a leader, you recognise you're probably better off doing something else or letting someone else step up.

If you're at this point, you've got three options:

1. Learn the skills you need to become a better leader for your organisation.
2. Take a step back and let someone else do it.
3. Just carry on as you are.

If you chose number three, I urge you to take a moment and think about it. If you're adamant you don't need to change or improve, then at least have some people around you that can support you on this journey. If you're not a people person, find someone who is. If you struggle with numbers, find someone who loves them.

LEARNING

“

BE WILLING TO LEARN AND BE OPEN TO EVERY SINGLE DIFFERENT POINT OF VIEW as nobody has the ultimate truth.

—Carlos Andres Posada Lopez

LEARNING

1. YOU'LL NEVER KNOW IT ALL

You can't think you know everything about leadership. Good leaders can be humble and admit to not knowing stuff: 'I don't know this, can you help me out?' But traditional leaders see that as a weakness and find it tough to do; they think they know everything. After all, if it's worked historically for them and it's got them to where they are now, why shouldn't it work in the future? But as you know, changes are coming. 'People Power' is huge and they'll vote with their feet if leaders don't change, don't adapt and don't learn.

All of the accidental leaders I spoke to in the course of writing this book mention learning as a critical part of their leadership: Carlos lists learning as the first piece of advice he'd give to new leaders; Mickela is constantly learning from her mentors; and Marc admits that part of becoming a good leader meant having to learn a lot more about himself in the process.

One of my clients, Luis, used to be a leader but had left that behind when he came to me for coaching. He had no ambitions to return to leadership, but every two weeks he would still have a session with me where I would tell him exactly what I was teaching other people. It was a way for him to keep learning about leadership, even though he had a completely different job. He didn't want to forget how to think or act like a leader and wanted to hear other leaders' challenges – even if he wasn't going to do it himself. And so he worked with me just to keep himself informed.

That's an unusual example, but the message is the same. It's critical that you realise there will never come a point at which you can say you know everything there is to know about leadership. Instead, constantly find ways to better yourself.

One of my first (and best) bosses once said to me, 'Stay in a job because you're having fun or learning – ideally both. But money alone isn't a reason to stay.' It's a mantra I've stuck to throughout my career and I pass it on to everyone who works for me. Make time to learn, read, listen and watch. It's part of being a great leader, not a luxury or guilty pleasure. That constant desire to become a better version of yourself is what will make you a REAL. leader – it's an essential leadership skill. Leadership is changing, so learning has never been more important.

STEP 1. **HAVE THE HUMILITY TO REALISE YOU DON'T KNOW EVERYTHING ABOUT LEADERSHIP; KEEP LEARNING FROM EVERYONE, ANYWHERE.**

STEP 2. **DON'T HAVE BIASES ABOUT WHO YOU CAN LEARN FROM OR WHAT YOU NEED TO LEARN.**

STEP 3. **SHARE WHAT YOU LEARN. IT WILL BE USEFUL FOR YOUR TEAM AND THEY WILL RESPOND IN KIND.**

“

LEARN OR HAVE FUN
or leave.

2. DON'T CALL YOURSELF A LEADER

You might be in a position of authority, but does that mean you're an effective leader? People mistakenly believe that unless they have the title they can't manage or lead others, and that once they have the title it will suddenly fall into place. But, when I spoke to Pete Wallroth about his transition into leadership, he believed that, 'There is an element of leading that can happen without it ever being in name.' You don't need the title to be a great leader. In the same way, just because you have the title, doesn't mean you are a leader, and Pete's experienced this first-hand by doing it himself.

If you really want to be a great leader, prove it. The best leaders start off by stepping up and 'assuming' the role before it's given. Step in and help out the current leader, start to separate yourself from your peers, seek out mentors and development, and take on extra responsibility. Perhaps even mentor your peers.

For me, the easiest way to make someone a good manager or leader is when they've already assumed the role. If everyone sees you as leadership material and are willing to be led by you, you'll be the obvious choice when the next promotion becomes available. It's like earning your stripes.

LEADERSHIP IS NOT ABOUT HAVING A TITLE. IT'S ABOUT HOW PEOPLE REACT AND RESPOND TO YOU – THAT'S WHAT MAKES YOU A LEADER.

Being a leader is about more than just your title, it's about how you're perceived by others. In this book I've talked about teachers or nurses as examples of leaders, and it's the reason I've featured 'Everyday Leaders' as examples. They earned their leadership rather than waiting for it to be given to them.

"

YOU'RE NOT ALLOWED TO CALL YOURSELF A LEADER. THAT'S LIKE CALLING YOURSELF FUNNY OR GOOD-LOOKING.

It's other people who decide whether or not you are someone they want to follow. If they look at you as a leader, then you are a leader. Otherwise, you're just in charge.

—Rich Diviney, Retired Navy Seal Commander

3. HUMILITY

If someone comes to your organisation and has a poor experience, who's responsible for that?

YOU.

Even if you weren't present for the experience, it's on you: you didn't design the product properly, didn't invest in training, didn't hire the right people, or didn't listen to those around you. Having humility is realising that you will always make mistakes and you will always be learning. There is no merit in saying you've got all the answers, because you haven't – and everyone knows that.

Bad leaders will have a lack of humility and a lack of wanting to learn. They'll just think, 'Oh, if I just tweak the way I've done things, I'll still survive, and I'll be brilliant.' Meanwhile, their whole industry is changing beneath them and they wonder why their leadership is beginning to struggle. Then they'll say, 'Let's talk to someone who's going to challenge us.' But they don't actually like the fact they're being challenged and ignore what they learn.

Humility is knowing *when* you've got to learn something, and being comfortable enough to *want* to learn it, whether that's from someone more junior than you, someone you don't like, or someone you never dreamed of learning from.

When I spoke to Alex Stephany, he admitted that he still has so much more to learn. He is constantly being educated by the people he exists to serve, the people he works with and others in his sector. 'Understanding your strengths and weaknesses – particularly as a purpose-driven leader – is crucial,' he says.

Humility in leadership is realising you're not the most important person in the room, and your role will always be to facilitate the success of others and your organisation. To do that you have to be willing to keep learning.

STEP 1. **DEVELOP THE SELF-AWARENESS TO UNDERSTAND WHERE AND WHAT YOU NEED TO LEARN.**

STEP 2. **CONTROL YOUR EGO AND YOUR PRIDE. ASK THE QUESTIONS YOU NEED TO ASK, EVEN IF THEY'RE STUPID.**

STEP 3. **LEARN FROM THE RIGHT PEOPLE. DON'T GO TO THE 'YES' PEOPLE, GO TO THE PEOPLE WHO WILL CHALLENGE YOU AND PUSH YOU TO BE BETTER.**

4. LEADING THROUGH UNCERTAINTY

The year is 2004. It's the Olympic Games and they're being held in Athens, Greece. Up next is synchronised diving. The Greeks weren't known for being the greatest divers and they were up against some of the best from all over the world: the Americans, the Chinese, the British.

On the day of the finals the competitors are lining up to do their final dives. Suddenly, a spectator jumps out of the crowd, dressed in a tutu and polka dot tights, and leaps off the 3-metre diving board screaming, 'I love you!' You can imagine the chaos.

Eventually, they get him out and the whole competition starts again.

First up are the Chinese ... but they completely fail their dive. Then the Russian pair got up ... and completely failed their dive. Then the Americans, the same. Then it got to the Greeks.

The Greeks got the best dives that day.[13]

Why?

All those other nations trained in these perfectly sanitised, multimillion-dollar environments. They never had weird things happen to them during training. But for the Greeks, it was just another day. They were used to sharing their training pool with the public. Interruptions were nothing new. And even though this was a huge day for them, they didn't let it bother them.

The reason I like this example is because it doesn't matter how great you are, how much you've trained, or how many things I tell you, the reality is you can't control the things that will throw you off. But you *can* control how you react to them. Everyone but the Greeks let the interruption get to them and throw them off their dives. So how will you react when something unexpected happens?

A friend of mine runs an online events company. Whenever something goes wrong they immediately email all the attendees and say, 'We're really sorry for the technical problems. But to make up for it, you're going to get your favourite chocolate bar, just tell us what it is.' It's really funny because you get a great response – people love free chocolate. And it's a great way to manage uncertainty.

13 Diving at the 2004 Summer Olympics – Men's synchronized 3 metre springboard – Wikipedia

WHEN THINGS AREN'T GOING WELL THAT'S THE OPTIMUM TIME TO THINK ABOUT BUILDING UP YOUR TEAM AND MOTIVATING THEM. HOW CAN YOU CREATE AND STRENGTHEN THAT TEAM ENVIRONMENT AND HELP THEM FEEL PART OF SOMETHING?

Even if you don't yet have a solution to the problem, be transparent and let them know you're working on it and what you're doing to get there. Put yourself in their shoes.

5. THE 'AWARE BUT DON'T CARE' EXCUSE

It really annoys me when people say, 'I know I've got to change,' or 'Sorry, I did it again,' but then they never make any effort to do so. If you're fully aware of your weaknesses, and proudly tell everyone about how self-aware you are, but then do nothing about it, that's far worse than someone who simply doesn't realise.

I've had clients like this who have come to me for help because they don't understand why they aren't progressing, or why their team doesn't respect them. Once I start coaching them, I can see where the problems lie and I encourage them to take action – but they don't. They say, 'Steve, I'm really sorry I forgot to do that'. or 'I'm aware of what I did,' but then don't change. It's at this point when I usually tell them they're wasting their money because coaching will never work for them.

"

The aware but don't care excuse – **EASIER TO KEEP SAYING SORRY THAN MAKING THE EFFORT TO CHANGE BEHAVIOUR.**

Don't come to me and ask me for advice or support if you're not going to do anything with it. Don't read books, or take courses, or have coaching if you're not going to action it. Leaders who are 'aware but don't care' will be seen as all talk and no action. Eventually, your leadership will fail because no one's going to trust you, no one will want to be led by you, and no one will come to you when it matters most.

This goes for people in your senior team, too. If someone behaves like this, but never changes, issue an ultimatum: take corrective action, stop doing it or face the consequences.

LEADERSHIP ISN'T ABOUT YOU. IT'S ABOUT HOW OTHER PEOPLE EXPERIENCE YOUR LEADERSHIP. IF YOU'RE AWARE YOU HAVE A PARTICULAR WEAKNESS OR BEHAVIOUR THAT'S WRONG, THEN CHANGE IT. IF YOU'RE AWARE, AND YOU DON'T DO ANYTHING ABOUT IT – YOU KEEP SAYING 'SORRY, IT'S JUST WHO I AM.' – THAT'S POOR LEADERSHIP AND YOU SHOULDN'T BE IN THAT ROLE.

EDUCATION

EDUCATION

1. LEADERSHIP REHEARSALS

You're constantly being watched, wherever you are and whatever you do, so it amazes me how many leaders don't prepare. You don't get a chance to make many mistakes. How many times have you left meetings or presentations wishing you'd said something different? Or wishing you hadn't acted a certain way? Everyone does that; I probably did it this morning.

So if you get the chance to practise and rehearse a situation, why wouldn't you? It's about testing things out and getting feedback before you go in. A lot of people don't want to do this, maybe they feel awkward or embarrassed, but I think it's important. This is about making sure those mistakes don't happen. It's not about rehearsing it perfectly. Life isn't scripted and it'll never go exactly to plan, but it's about being prepared.

One of my clients, Emily, had to do a presentation to the board as their new CEO. We were having our usual coaching sessions and she said, 'It's really stressing me out.'

'OK, why don't you let me have a look at it?' I suggested.

'You know about sales?' she said, surprised.

Once I'd explained that I'd actually started my career in sales, I said, 'Let's look at your presentation and pretend I'm your new boss. Imagine I want to see it now, not next week. How would you do it?'

'OK,' she said, 'but it won't be as good.'

At the end of the roleplay, I gave her feedback and told her exactly what I thought: it *was* good and she didn't need to do any more work on it. It gave her the freedom to start thinking about other ways she could provide value in the presentation, and what the next steps could be.

Just think about how many times you've walked out of a situation wishing you'd said or done something different, this is a chance to maybe stop that happening. If you think about it like that, why wouldn't you practise it first?

STEP 1. **HAVE SOMEONE YOU CAN ROLEPLAY WITH. SOMEONE YOU'RE COMFORTABLE WITH AND THAT YOU TRUST.**

STEP 2. **TREAT IT LIKE THE REAL THING. HAVE A SENSE OF URGENCY. PRETEND THE CALL GOT MOVED TO TODAY, OR YOU HAVE TO FIRE SOMEONE NOW.**

STEP 3. **SOMETIMES, I SUGGEST PEOPLE RECORD THEMSELVES AND WATCH IT BACK. IT'S IMPORTANT THAT YOU SEE YOURSELF AS OTHERS SEE YOU. IT WILL FEEL HORRIBLE BUT TRY TO SEPARATE YOURSELF FROM WHAT YOU SEE AND BE LOGICAL ABOUT HOW YOU MIGHT COME ACROSS TO YOUR AUDIENCE.**

2. BECOME A HEAR-A-HOLIC

Most leaders listen, but do you actually hear what's being said? Do you know the difference? We've all been in those situations where the leader says, 'I really want to hear what everyone's got to say ...' but then nothing happens. They're listening, but they're not *hearing*. Hearing is when you actually do something about what's been said.

Unfortunately, there's an innate anxiety that leaders have when they come into a new role. They say, 'I'm going to listen, I want to learn from everyone,' but then they panic, thinking they have to prove their leadership by *doing* something, quickly. But the world of leadership has changed, and people now know that leaders have to listen – so give yourself time to do that. I suspect that the companies that haemorrhage staff, or can't attract new talent, are the ones where people realise they aren't being listened to and are moving on.

Notice who you give time to and who you don't. Notice if there are people you overlook. I once recorded a workshop I had hosted, and when I listened back I realised I hadn't actually been listening to everyone. The person who I thought didn't contribute very much actually made some amazing points, and I would have failed to notice if I hadn't listened again.

Enable people to use their voice and create an environment where everyone has the confidence and tools to voice themselves in whatever way works for them.

You need to become a 'Hear-a-holic'. I love this phrase because that's exactly what needs to happen. You need to always be hearing, rather than just sitting there passively listening.

STEP 1. **IF YOU'RE NEW TO LEADERSHIP, OR NEW TO A ROLE, COMMIT TO A PERIOD OF DOING NOTHING BUT LISTENING. YOU DON'T HAVE TO GO ONTO THE SHOP FLOOR BUT IT'S HIGHLY RECOMMENDED THAT YOU GET INTO THE WEEDS. COMMIT TO TIME WHERE ALL YOU'RE DOING IS LISTENING TO YOUR ORGANISATION AND LEARNING WHAT IT NEEDS.**

STEP 2. **IF SOMEONE HAS COME TO TALK TO YOU, GIVE THEM THE SPACE AND TIME THEY NEED. DON'T DOMINATE THE CONVERSATION; GIVE YOURSELF TIME TO THINK AND RESPOND. YOU SHOULD BE HEARING 80% OF THE TIME AND TALKING 20% OF THE TIME.**

STEP 3. **BE CAREFUL ABOUT HOW YOU REACT. AS WE'VE TALKED ABOUT BEFORE, SOMETIMES PEOPLE NEED TO VENT AND THAT'S FINE, YOU CAN JUST SIT THERE AND LISTEN. BUT OTHER TIMES, THEY ARE TALKING TO YOU BECAUSE THEY NEED YOU TO ACT AND THAT'S WHEN YOU NEED TO *HEAR* THEM.**

“

WHEN YOU TALK, YOU ARE ONLY REPEATING WHAT YOU ALREADY KNOW;

but if you listen you may learn something new.

—Dalai Lama

3. COACHING

Some of the best leaders in the world have coaches. Bill Campbell coached some of the biggest and most recognisable names in Silicon Valley. Top professional sports players have coaches, and even their managers have coaches. A coach doesn't have to be better than you at what you do, that's not their job. They're there to help you be better, find habits and skills you can tweak and suggest improvements. Coaches aren't invested in your business, they've invested in you, so why wouldn't you have someone help you improve? When I need help I speak to people who have nothing to do with my business because it's easy to become too insular and blinded by your own experience. My coach, who is also a mentor and friend, is an accomplished and very respected university professor in Chicago. He knows more about leadership and people theory than I will ever understand but he respects my experience and hands-on style. He keeps me very grounded in terms of focus and sticking to my values.

I also think that some of the best leaders *are* coaches, too. They have to read between the lines and help people find their own answers, and that's coaching. A common thing that comes up when I talk to teams, is that they wish their leader had more time to coach them. They wish they had more time to show them what they're good at or give them a peek behind the curtain at all the stuff they deal with – for example, strategy, politics, accounts. When a leader is inspiring, the team will always want more from them.

I asked Marc Convey to describe leadership. He sees it as finding what helps that 'individual to thrive'. He says it's about empowering that team member to take responsibility for their own future, because you can't hold their hand forever, and I think that's where coaching comes in as an essential skill for leaders. Whether you are the one doing it for your team, or being coached, REAL. leaders are always coaching and motivating their people. It's an important skill to have and it can help reinforce what you've already learned. When you pass on your knowledge to someone else, when you help your team and coach them to success, you realise just how much value you have and how much you've learned.

COACHING IS A GREAT WAY TO REINFORCE YOUR ROLE AS A LEADER; AND BEING COACHED HELPS YOU UNDERSTAND WHAT YOU'RE GOOD AT AND FEEL MORE CONFIDENT IN YOUR ROLE. YOU CAN WORK ON YOUR WEAKNESSES AND STRENGTHS AND FIND WAYS TO BE A BETTER LEADER. I THINK COACHING IS WHAT EMPLOYEES TYPICALLY WANT FROM THEIR LEADER. THEY WANT TO LEARN FROM AND BE GUIDED BY SOMEONE THAT INSPIRES THEM.

4. LEARN FROM YOUR JUNIORS

This is a fairly large topic so there are three key things I want to give you. The first is a story about Emma. Last year, I was coaching her because she was really worried about her communication style. She is a very stats-oriented leader and likes meetings with a lot of detail. But she was concerned she was missing an opportunity for team-building or motivation in her team meetings because it was so focused on the numbers. So, she changed it up – and surprisingly, got complaints.

After talking about it, I suggested she talk to the most junior members in her team and get their views. After all, they'd be the ones who'd be getting the message last, as everything cascades down and stops with them. When she pulled them aside and asked them about the changes, they said, 'Go back to the stats.' They could team-build in their own time, she didn't need to worry about motivation – what motivated them was hearing about how the rest of the business worked and seeing the stats. She didn't realise how much people appreciated her strengths as a numbers person and it validated this as a core part of her leadership style. But she wouldn't have known that if she hadn't checked in with the most junior members of the team.

The second is this: one of the best things I ever did, before I became a coach, was to tell the new recruits or the most junior people on my team, 'I'll give you the boring intro now, but in about two weeks' time, when you've spent a bit more time here, I'd love you to tell me what I'm doing wrong.' Do you know what they told me? That my presentations were boring, and they were too light on content. That I didn't give equal recognition for teamwork. I spent too much time with senior people. That I needed to share my vision and reassure people during turbulent times. It wasn't easy to hear, but it was critical and essential feedback that my immediate team probably wouldn't have told me otherwise.

You learn more from people who are not yet changed by your organisation than you do from people who are. If you give them a safe space to do so, you'll get lots of valuable feedback in return. It was a little thing to ask, but the feedback I got back was priceless.

The third thing I want to share is that when I was leading, I used to set up a group called the Change Agents. They were a group of three or four people who were voted in every year by their peers. They were people who had a voice among their team, and who others trusted and went to with their problems. Every month I would take these Change Agents to lunch and they had the freedom to tell me everything – and I mean *everything*. If I'd done something terrible, or something had happened, they told me. There was never any risk of retribution. It was a safe space for them, and I would listen and implement changes that were needed.

You can learn a lot from your juniors. Remember, your job is to lead and coordinate the success of others; you're a master at that. So, there's nothing wrong with saying to someone, 'You're fantastic at social media,' or 'You're a great communicator, I'd like to learn how to do that.' Someone I coached once asked me, 'Doesn't that make me look weak? Isn't it weird to admit "I'm not good at this"?' But good leadership is about having the humility to learn from people around you and below you, and I admire leaders who have the humility to do this – because not all of them do.

“

CHANGE AGENTS – appointing a team of junior people to challenge your leadership.

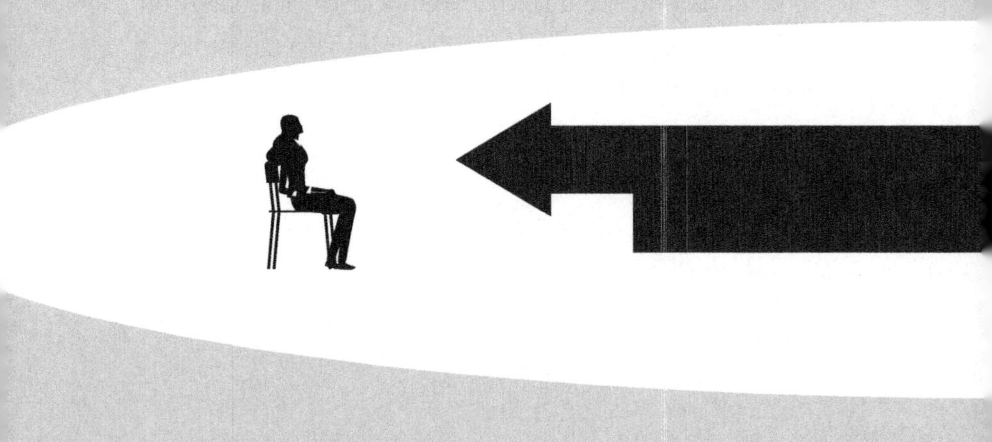

STEP 1. LEARNING DOESN'T ALWAYS HAVE TO COME FROM PEOPLE MORE SENIOR OR EXPERIENCED THAN YOU. HAVE THE HUMILITY TO SEEK OUT OPPORTUNITIES WITH PEOPLE YOU LEAD.

STEP 2. WHEN YOU ASK FOR PEOPLE'S TIME, IT'S A TWO-WAY THING. DO SOMETHING FOR THEM IN RETURN THAT SHOWS YOU APPRECIATED THEIR TIME.

STEP 3. AS A LEADER, YOUR JOB IS TO DECIDE WHAT YOU ARE GOING TO DO WITH THAT INFORMATION. WHAT IS THE RIGHT THING FOR YOUR ORGANISATION? ONCE YOU'VE LEARNED THAT NEW PIECE OF INFORMATION, TAKE THE TIME TO DECIDE WHAT YOU NEED TO IMPLEMENT AND WHAT YOU DON'T, BASED ON THE CONTEXT OF YOUR WORK.

STEP 4. NEVER USE WHAT YOU'VE LEARNED AGAINST YOUR TEAM OR AS LEVERAGE TO TURN EVERYTHING UPSIDE DOWN. YOU DON'T WANT PEOPLE TO START MISTRUSTING YOUR ATTEMPTS TO LEARN FROM THEM.

“

KRULAK’S LAW:
‘THE EXPERIENCE PEOPLE HAVE WITH YOUR BRAND IS IN THE HANDS OF THE PERSON YOU PAY THE LEAST.’

ACT ACCORDINGLY.

It mostly means seeing the front-line people in your organization as priceless assets, not cheap cogs.

—Seth Godin

5. THE STARS NEED YOU, TOO

If you look at the people you lead, you'll find about 20% of them are amazing, and they're your stars. Then you'll have the bottom 20%, the people you're constantly trying to motivate and push. And then there are those in the middle who are average; neither standing out nor struggling.

Most leaders spend their time helping the bottom 20%, but I want to remind them, and you, that you mustn't forget the people higher up.

The 'middling' people will need you because there's a chance one of them could become one of your stars. All they need is a push in the right direction to improve their skills or attitude, or maybe they just need to find their spark.

And those stars, the people who are already at the top of the organisation for amazing performance, still need you, too. I can guarantee if they're already at the top of the rankings, they're thinking, 'This is great, but what's next?' and other organisations will have noticed them, too. There's a trend in coaching, and in business, where we all tend to focus on problems, weaknesses and the gaps in our knowledge. But why not focus on what we're good at? Why not focus on the strengths of your top performers and make them even better, or ask them to coach others? If you look at what coaches do for sports people, it's always about improving an existing strength, like making a strong backhand even stronger, or a fast lap time even faster. If you spend all your time with the poorest performers, you'll find they take up not only your physical time but they drain your mental energy, too. Weaknesses may be something people might never be able to do, but strengths can always be improved.

You have a duty to keep everyone motivated, learning and developing. I always think of teachers when I think of this. They have to care about every student and find a way to level up the poor performers, while at the same time inspiring the top students, too. Teachers have to decide where to spend their time effectively and I think they're brilliant natural leaders.

STEP 1. **IF YOU'VE GOT SOMEONE WHO'S NOT PERFORMING, WHO YOU'RE CONSTANTLY JUSTIFYING TO OTHERS, ASK YOURSELF WHY YOU TOLERATE THAT PERSON. IF THEY CAN'T IMPROVE, OR DON'T WANT TO, SHOULD THEY STAY?**

STEP 2. **IF YOU'VE GOT SOMEONE WHO'S AVERAGE, OR MEDIOCRE, HOW CAN YOU HELP IMPROVE THEIR RESULTS? HOW CAN YOU HELP THEM BE MORE ENTHUSIASTIC ABOUT THEIR ROLE? WHAT DO THEY NEED?**

STEP 3. **MAKE SURE YOU'RE DEVELOPING PEOPLE AT THE TOP. PLAN OUT YOUR ORGANISATION: KNOW WHO AND WHERE YOUR PEOPLE ARE AND WHERE YOU WANT THEM TO END UP. THEN CREATE A PLAN TO HELP THEM GET THERE.**

6. THE BUS EXERCISE

Here's a taster of another exercise that I've picked up:[14]

Think of your business as a bus. You're the driver and your passengers are the ones who will help you get to your destination. But there are challenges to driving this bus:

1. Your passengers might not be the right people you need to get you, or your organisation, to the next destination.
2. Perhaps you've got the right people on the bus, but they're in the wrong seat.
3. You might have passengers coming on board too early, and you don't have the right seats for them.
4. Maybe you have passengers who have been in the same seats for far too long.

Map out the bus as your organisation currently stands and see where your people fit. Then ask yourself:

1. Is this the perfect seating arrangement or structure for your business or does something need to change?
2. Who do you want in this role, or that role? What are the qualities they will need? What will they be doing?
3. Who needs training?
4. Does someone need to move seats?
5. Has someone come on board too early, and you're not ready for them yet?

14 Jim Collins, (2001). Good to Great: Why Some Companies Make the Leap … And Others Don't.

I encourage you to verbalise this idea with your team, especially if you've got some big changes coming. This isn't about looking for people to throw off the bus, it's about planning your perfect organisation, which takes time. It's a really pivotal exercise and it took me a year to go through the process after I'd originally mapped it out. But it meant in that year, I got the right people in the right 'seats' for the business. I learned about who the organisation needed and discovered how to make it even better.

When you build a business or grow an organisation, the people that got it to where it is today probably aren't going to be the same people who'll get it to the next phase. And that could include you, as the leader. It's a tough exercise but it's important to do.

STEP 1. TAKE THE EMOTION OUT OF THIS. THIS IS A LOGICAL EXERCISE AND YOU HAVE TO BE ABLE TO THINK CLEARLY ABOUT PEOPLE AND THEIR ROLES.

STEP 2. STICK TO YOUR DECISION. IT'S EASY TO BE SWAYED OR CHANGE YOUR MIND, ESPECIALLY IF YOU ARE CLOSE TO YOUR TEAM, BUT YOU HAVE TO STAY TRUE TO YOUR DECISION.

STEP 3. DON'T RUSH. THIS IS NOT AN OVERNIGHT CHANGE, IT WILL TAKE TIME.

“

LEADERS ARE FOOTBALL MANAGERS
or orchestra conductors.

7. THE FOOTBALL MANAGER AND ORCHESTRA CONDUCTOR

You can think of leadership like being a football manager; you don't have to be the best player on the field to be the best football manager. Or if football isn't your thing, it's like being an orchestra conductor; you don't have to be the best violinist to be able to conduct an orchestra.

Your job is to manage and guide that talent towards achieving the group vision. And that means managing people who might be far more skilled than you at doing what they do.

Carlos Posada once had a web developer who was far more experienced and knowledgeable about tech than he was. But that member of staff was overstepping their role. They were upsetting the team, challenging the leadership and ruining relationships Carlos had built with other farms. I had to remind Carlos to take a step back and realise that while he may not be an expert at tech, that didn't matter because he was still the leader of that organisation. We went through all the possible scenarios and roleplayed how to end the working relationship. It didn't matter what the team member said, what he did, how angry or emotional he became, Carlos stuck to the plan.

As a leader you may feel insecure because you're working with amazingly talented and experienced people. You will be challenged by people who are more skilled or confident than you. But you need to realise that you're in that leadership role for a reason. You bring something to the table that they can't, and you need to be comfortable communicating and demonstrating that.

STEP 1. **PEOPLE WILL CHALLENGE YOUR LEADERSHIP, BUT STAY CALM WHILE SETTING AND ENFORCING YOUR BOUNDARIES.**

STEP 2. **MAKE IT CLEAR WHAT YOU BRING TO THE TABLE. FROM YOUR FIRST INTERACTION WITH A NEW TEAM, TO YOUR FIRST ONE-TO-ONE. HELP THEM UNDERSTAND WHY YOU ARE THE LEADER SO THERE IS NO CONFUSION.**

STEP 3. **CONSTANTLY MAKE SURE YOU HAVE THE RIGHT PEOPLE IN THE RIGHT ROLES. MAKE SURE THEY ARE UP TO DATE WITH THEIR SKILLS AND HELP THEM MAKE THE BEST OF THEIR POSITION.**

"

DON'T THINK OF LEADERSHIP AS A BIG TITLE AND BEING ABLE TO BOSS A LOT OF PEOPLE AROUND. It is actually having a course and sticking to it. Leading a debate on something, bringing people along with you and having a vision about the future. That comes from within.

—Sandie Okoro, Senior VP and General Counsel at the World Bank

8. CHOOSE YOUR SUCCESSOR

Imagine a scenario where you win the lottery tomorrow … and you take the money and run. What happens to your organisation, to your team and work you've done? Who steps up?

The critical part of any business or organisation, if it's going to scale and grow, is to find a successor. And by successor, I mean someone that can step in and do your role at short notice – and then eventually take over your role when you leave. It annoys me when I hear people who've left their organisation or been fired, proudly say, 'Well, of course it all went wrong when I left.' That's not good leadership. Whatever happens, the business should never ever fold without you. Great leadership is about creating an environment that is successful even when you're not there. So, put your ego aside and think about who your successor could be. How would you define that person? What do they need to learn? What do you need to share with them?

But what if you don't want to hire someone in case they could do your job? What if people prefer them over you? Think of it this way: how do sports people climb the ranks and win? They play people who are equal to, or better than them. If you want to improve in your leadership, bring in people who are going to challenge you. Sometimes, finding your successor means finding someone who's better than you at running your organisation.

It'll be a challenging learning process because you'll discover more about yourself and what's right for your business than you expect. But being a REAL. leader means understanding where your strengths and weaknesses lie and being humble enough to know the right time to step out.

STEP 1. **DON'T FIND ONE SUCCESSOR, FIND TWO OR THREE. AND THEN FIND THEIR SUCCESSOR, TOO. IF THEY STEP UP TO HELP YOU, SOMEONE'S GOT TO TAKE THEIR PLACE. REMEMBER, YOU'RE CREATING AN ENVIRONMENT FOR SUCCESS.**

STEP 2. **YOUR SUCCESSOR MAY NOT BE THE FINISHED ARTICLE WHEN YOU FIRST MEET THEM. YOU'VE GOT TO THINK ABOUT HOW YOU'RE GOING TO COACH OR MENTOR THEM, AND HOW YOU'RE GOING TO GET THEM READY.**

STEP 3. **YOU'RE NEVER LOOKING FOR A MIRROR IMAGE OF YOURSELF. THAT WOULDN'T IMPROVE THE BUSINESS. YOU WANT TO FIND SOMEONE WHO'S LIKE YOU – BUT BETTER.**

THE FIFTH PILLAR

“

LIFE IS LIKE RIDING A BICYCLE. To keep your balance, you must keep moving.

—Albert Einstein

THE FIFTH PILLAR

1. THE FIFTH PILLAR

Someone once told me I needed to open up more because my team wanted to know more about me. But I really wasn't comfortable with that. I liked keeping some aspects of my life private and that's OK, it's my choice to do so. However, with that decision I had to recognise if this is where I'm going to draw the line, my team might not get everything they need from me as their leader. So, it's on me to find other ways to make it work for them.

You will always have to think about the other side of that line you've just drawn. Think of it as constantly balancing the scales. Everything you do in this role, the way you communicate, your tone of voice, what you say, how you act, where you work, what you wear, how you feel – there's got to be a balance. And that's why balance is the central pillar that ties everything together.

You've got to get results for your organisation and team, but you've got to balance the results against those you want to achieve for yourself. You've got to be empathetic so your team feels safe with you, but not overly so, that you lose objectivity and can't lead effectively. A balance of being authentic, but not so much that you feel uncomfortably vulnerable. And you need to find a balance in learning: knowing when to ask for help, and when to just get on with the job and make a decision. When to listen and when to take action.

Finally, there is work-life balance, we all know about that. As a leader, it's tempting to over-work as you want to set an example, to always be there for your team no matter what. But what happens if you get ill? What if you can't work? What would that mean? Leaders at work are often the leaders outside work, too, relied upon by many and with significant responsibilities. Often in our eagerness to support everyone around us, at work and at home, we forget ourselves; neglecting the essential 'me' time that we all need, doing something purely for ourselves.

The beautiful thing about balance is that it depends on you; where you're comfortable and what it is you want to do. Fundamentally you will lead based on who you are: your inherent strengths, capabilities and what you love doing. There is an element to being coached to help you find a better balance, but you've got to be comfortable with it – it's got to feel right.

You always have to be thinking about the other side of that line. If you express an opinion or take a stand on an issue you have to think, 'OK, is there anyone who I might have alienated right now? Is there anyone who might not see it this way?' You need self-awareness and to know there is always someone or something weighing in on the other side of those scales.

IF SOMEONE COMES TO YOU AND SAYS YOUR LEADERSHIP IS LACKING IN SOME WAY, PERHAPS YOU'RE NOT AUTHENTIC ENOUGH OR YOU'RE TOO RESULTS-FOCUSED, TAKE TIME TO FIND THE BALANCE. DON'T BE REACTIVE BUT FIND OUT WHY THEY THINK THIS. HOW DO OTHER PEOPLE VIEW YOU? HOW DO OTHER PEOPLE EXPERIENCE YOU? BE EMPATHETIC AND LISTEN. LEARN, AND THEN MAKE THE ADJUSTMENT BASED ON WHAT YOU DISCOVER.

2. THREE FROGS

Three frogs are on a log.

One frog decides to jump in the water.

How many frogs are left on the log?

... Three.

As this parable shows, *deciding is not doing.* If you finish reading this book, having made notes and thinking about what you're going to change, the reality is not a lot will. Thinking about it is not the same as doing it.

It's a common thing for people in leadership roles to worry, listen to people, be empathetic, and learn, but never actually get stuff done. All of the advice I've given you will help, but you've got to be aware that you won't always get it right. You might take it to an extreme and get it wrong, or not take it far enough. But that doesn't mean you shouldn't try. Again, it comes down to finding that balance in the way you want to learn and you can only figure it out by doing it.

As I've said time and time again, if you get something wrong – which you will – how will you act to fix it? When you overstep the mark, what will you do? That's the key thing. But if you don't try to improve or change it, don't be surprised if those leadership worries never disappear.

AFTER PUTTING THIS BOOK DOWN, TRY AND FOCUS ON ONE OR TWO THINGS YOU CAN ACTUALLY ACT ON BECAUSE THAT IS WHAT WILL CEMENT THESE IDEAS IN YOUR MIND. ONCE YOU'VE DONE THOSE, AND YOU ARE COMFORTABLE WITH THOSE IMPROVEMENTS, FIND ONE OR TWO MORE. DECIDE ON CHANGE AND THEN DO IT – DON'T STOP.

3. EVOLVING AS A LEADER

Leadership isn't fixed, you will evolve but it will always be about finding balance. What you might think is reasonable one day, might not work a few months down the line. It's OK to change your boundaries. But be ready to change, constantly. You will change as a person and as a leader, and so will your team. You have to remain curious, and want to learn new things so you can stay agile and adapt; sometimes that means changing the balance and moving that line. Finding that balance will be an essential part of your leadership as you evolve. The more experienced you get the easier it will be to find that balance.

THERE'S A REASON I STRONGLY ENCOURAGE LEARNING AND NETWORKING AS PART OF YOUR LEADERSHIP, BECAUSE THE MORE YOU LEARN AND THE LONGER YOU LEAD, THE MORE YOU'LL REALISE JUST HOW COMMON THIS ELEMENT OF LEADERSHIP IS. IT'S NOT FOUND JUST AMONG PEOPLE IN BUSINESS, BUT IN OTHER AREAS LIKE SPORT, ENTERTAINMENT, MEDICINE, EDUCATION AND ART.

4. FINAL THOUGHTS (OR LANDING THE PLANE)

When leadership is poor and people don't feel safe or cared for, that's when you start to see large social movements, civil unrest and people questioning and re-examining culture. We know this from our history books. You only have to check your social media accounts for the latest symptom of poor leadership manifesting as a wave of social unrest. The Great Resignation or Quiet Quitting may be trendy as I write this book, but it's just another symptom of leadership gone wrong. When people don't trust their leaders to deliver results, or don't believe they're as authentic or empathetic as they claim to be, people see no choice but to take the law into their own hands. We can see plenty of examples in the daily news of leaders who are lacking in one or more of the REAL. Pillars I've mentioned in this book.

Perhaps it's down to a lot of leaders feeling paralysed by these issues. There is no playbook for leadership anymore,

“

LEADERSHIP ISN’T FIXED, you will evolve but always need to find balance.

and the old traditional leaders are struggling. Expressing an opinion can open you up to criticism, decisions that come from a genuinely good place can sometimes backfire. No wonder there's a belief that a lot of leaders are not in touch with the issues of today.

But that's why learning is such an essential part of leadership. Why being humble, being authentic and everything else I've talked about in this book is so important. We need good leadership – new leadership – and that means trying things that haven't been done before. Looking to people who wouldn't consider themselves leaders, but just naturally are. Or giving traditional leaders the space to say, 'OK, I've messed up. I need to change.'

If you're struggling with how to lead in a difficult situation it comes back to being aware that everything you say – and everything you believe – you'll be on the hook for. You need to crystallise what your politics, your beliefs and your values are, and be very clear about standing by them. Leadership today is about transparency and building a personal brand. Professional and personal are all tied together now, and a lot of that is down to the 'People Power' that I mentioned at the start of this book. I'm a huge advocate of people being honest and open about how they lead, and people want insight into leader's lives these days, which they didn't have before. But this is where we have to talk again about drawing the line and finding balance. You don't want to be forcing your views on your team in terms of what you believe in. But you also have to be quite firm in how your business is going to progress and what that means when responding to external cultural and political influences. Find the balance that works for you and stick to it.

YOU'RE NOT ALONE

All I really want is for you is to read this book and know you're not alone. The questions you have and the fears you feel happen to everybody. Just find that one thing you can action after reading this book and I promise it'll be worth it.

We're all learning as we go, including me. I'm not a world qualified coach, but I have had more leadership experience than most people. I've done and learned a lot of things that I think are relevant and I wanted to tell you about them. Everything you've read is based on my beliefs from 30 years of talking to people, practising and getting things wrong, from failure and success and everything else that comes with this journey. There's a quote I love from Leena Nair, the Global CEO of Chanel, who once said, 'We're all in the same storm, but we're not in the same boat.' All I'm doing here is telling you how it is to be in one of these boats. But your boat is different to mine.

This book will never really be finished. There are always going to be things I want to add as I keep learning. But that's what leadership is, something that is never finished but constantly changing, growing and evolving. I hope you can feel reassured by that.

MY TEN PRINCIPLES OF REAL. LEADERSHIP

REAL. LEADERSHIP

1. People will follow what you do, more than what you say, so you need to live that, every day.
2. You need to get results, but you can only do that with a great team around you.
3. People always come first; the most important person is the one in front of you.
4. Stay humble when it all goes well, give sincere recognition and celebrate together.
5. Be honest when you need advice, don't know the answer, or simply find things tough.
6. Be authentic, you can't switch it on or off, be fair and equitable.
7. You don't know it all, listen and learn from everyone, anywhere, all the time.
8. Be flexible and embrace uncertainty.
9. Recruit people who are better than you and challenge you.
10. Learn, have fun or leave.

THANKS

Firstly, I'd like to thank the colleagues and friends who made some amazing contributions – Pete Wallroth, Mickela Hall-Ramsay, Alex Stephany, Dr Eunice Ndirangu-Mugo, Marc Convey and Carlos Andres Posada Lopez – all inspirational leaders in your own way.

I'd like to thank my coach/mentor/friend Bob Tenuta, you've been with me on this journey through thick and thin, always providing that reassuring voice of reason that kept me focused. And most importantly, you've challenged me to be true to myself.

I'd like to thank Mark and the team at NEO, the business creative agency, for the beautiful illustrations.

Finally, I'd like to thank Clare, my marketing partner for her amazing support as we've got this business off the ground, and Corinna for convincing me to write this book and then helping me to make it happen!

ABOUT THE AUTHOR

Steve Charlton is a transformational leadership coach and the founder of the REAL. Leadership Consultancy. In 2022 his business was voted one of the top leadership development coaching companies in the UK. He spent almost 25 years working in a variety of leadership roles and was a trustee of a charity called BSignificant, which trains and develops charity leaders to become more effective. He has also provided pro bono support as part of the EthicalCoach organisation. He has worked with leaders in a variety of sectors – from food to technology – in countries as diverse as Colombia and the Philippines and helped them to become better leaders. Steve currently lives in the UK. When he's not coaching he's trying to improve his triathlon times or walking his dog!

realleadership.consulting

Get
REAL.